THE
OLGA & FOLKE
PICTURE BOOK

Cover design by Leif Södergren

ISBN 978-91-979188-5-5

Special thanks to Torsten Atterbom

LEMONGULCHBOOKS
www.lemongulchbooks.com

The
Olga & Folke
Picture Book

By
Leif Södergren

To the memory
of my grandparents

CONTENTS

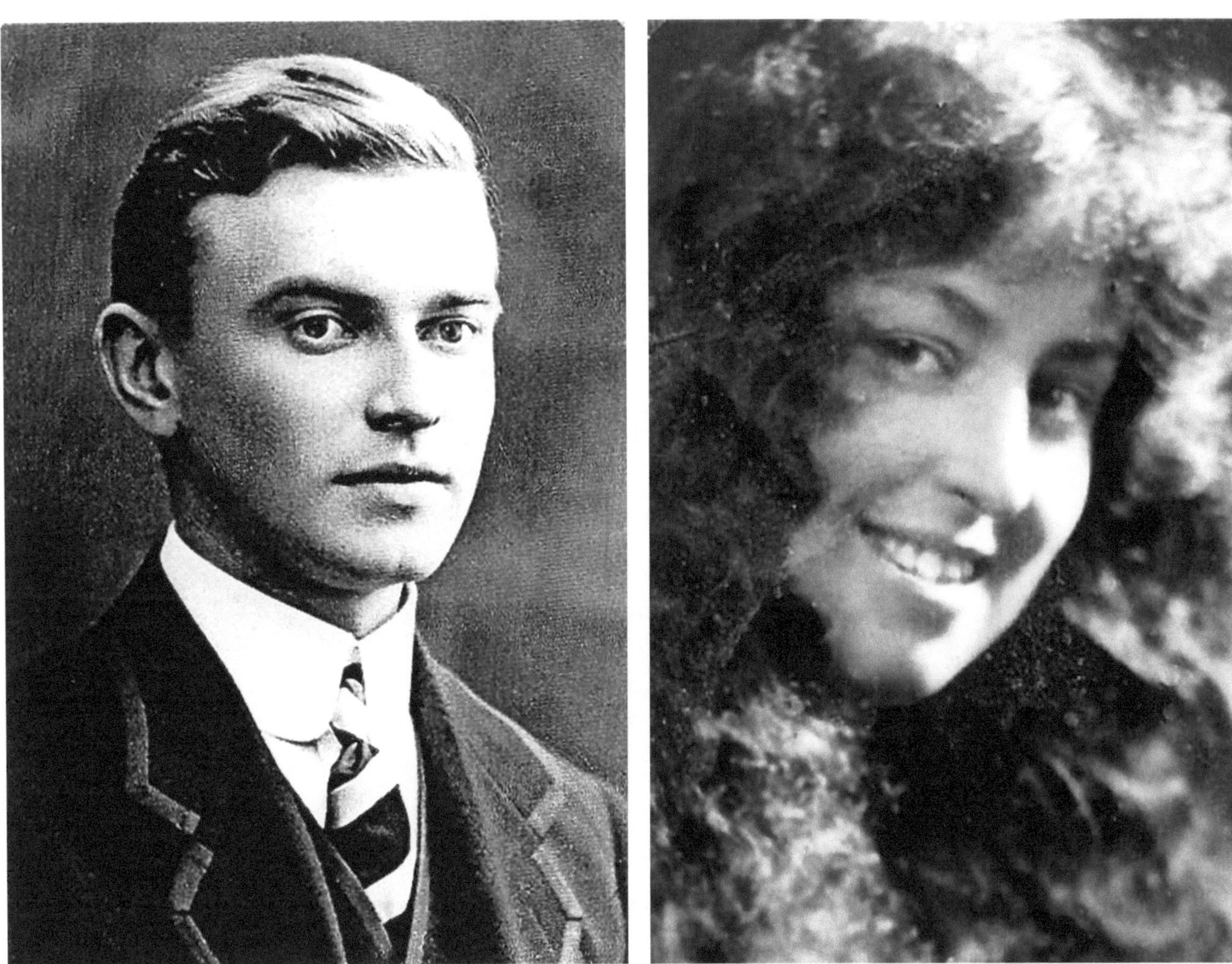

1909
ENGAGED TO BE MARRIED

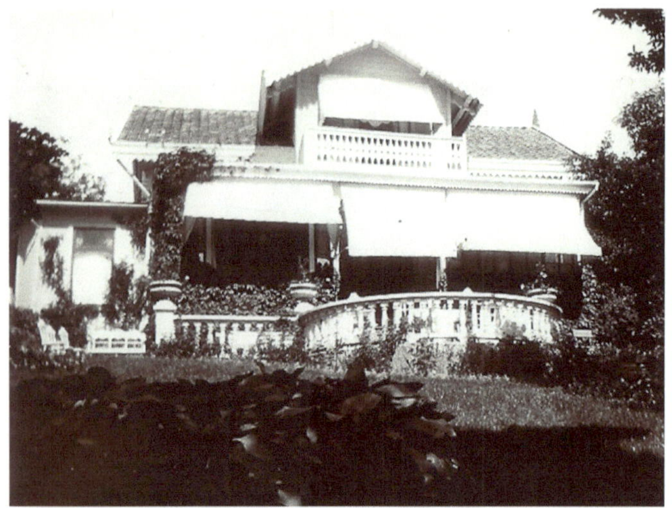

GETTING TO KNOW YOU

Once Olga's parents had agreed to the wedding and the engagement was a fact, Olga and her family, her father William Dawson, her mother Anita Ball Dawson, her sister Una and her brother Willie, all went to Sweden to meet Folke's Swedish family. They spent most of the summer of 1909 at Särö, the exclusive seaside resort outside Gothenburg on the Swedish West coast.

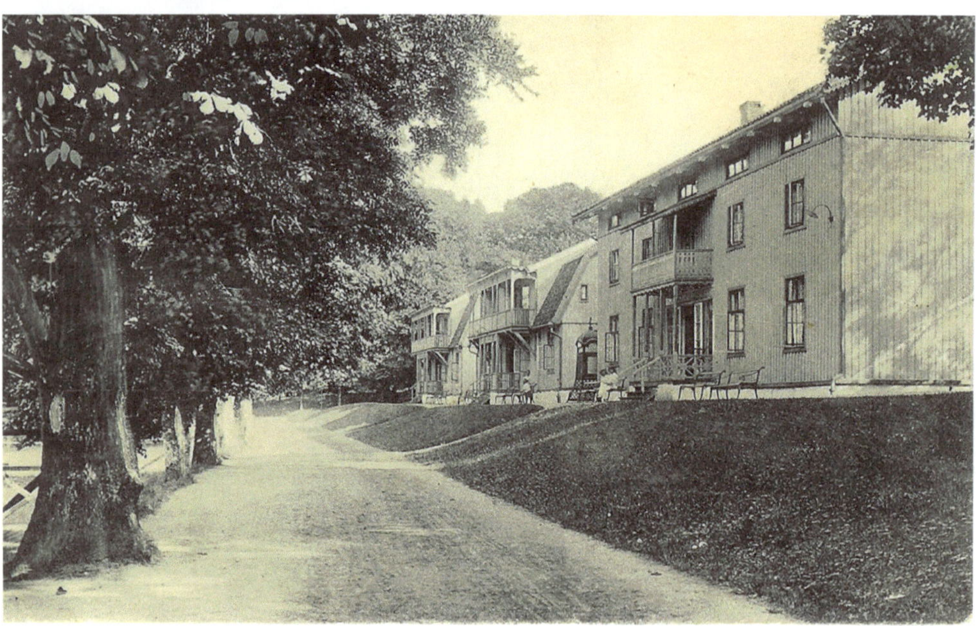

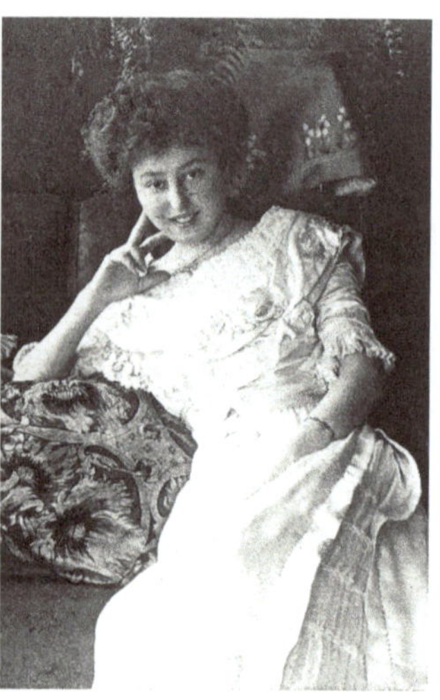

This is where Olga and her family rented three rooms and a balcony for the summer, to get acquainted with Folke's family. The two families got along very well and they all looked forward to the marriage in Paris that same year. Folke's father, Axel Jonsson lived nearby in villa "Beau Rivage" (top left)

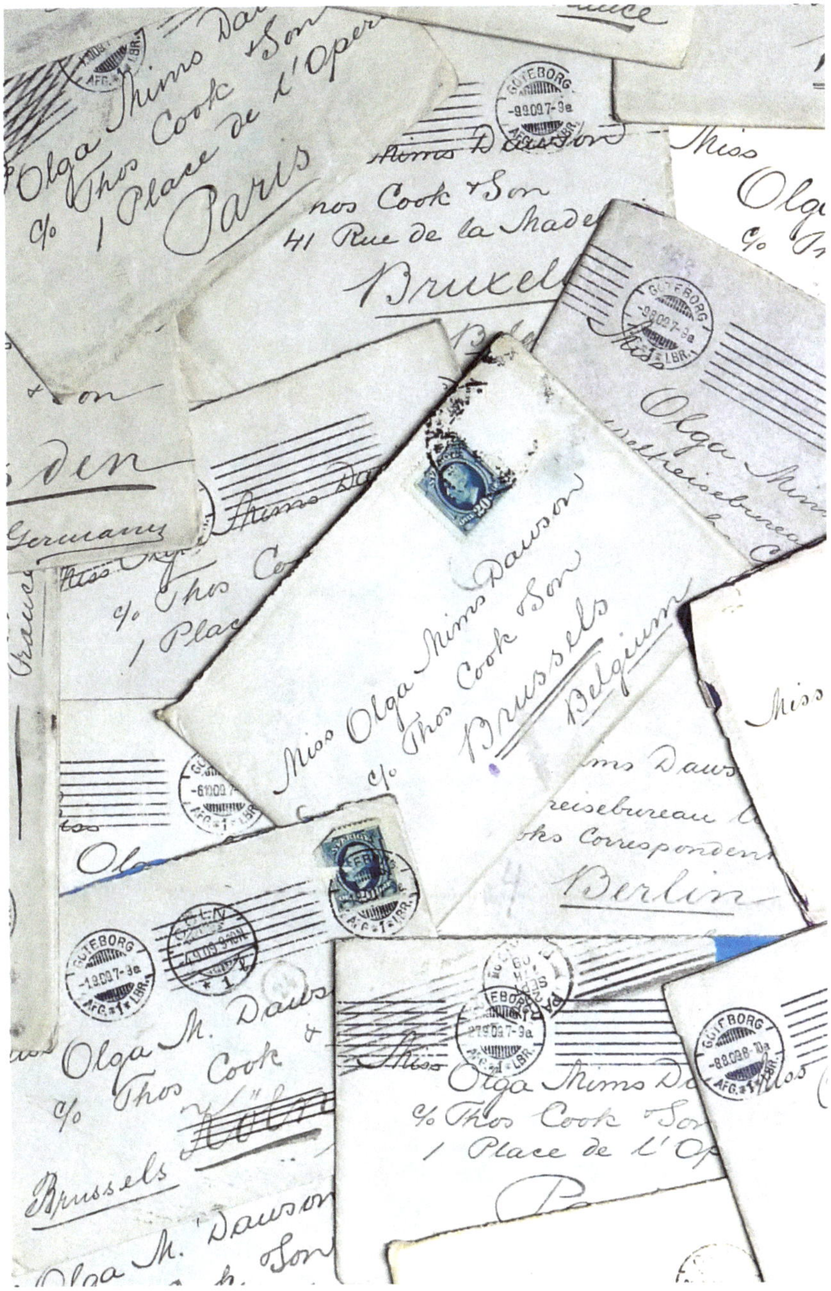

SEE YOU IN PARIS, DARLING OLGA!

The wedding was set for October in Paris. Olga and her family left in August to travel in Europe and arrange for the wedding. Folke remained in Sweden working for his father's company, Jonsson, Sternhagen & Co. This meant he would be without his beloved Olga for over two months and he wrote to her nearly every day. The addresses on the envelopes were c/o Thomas Cook in Germany, Belgium and France. Two months separation is a long time for two young people in love.

A ROSE FOR OLGA

SÄRÖ
AUGUST 11, 1909

Folke longed enormously for Olga and sent her a rose from Särö where they had been so happy that summer. He kissed it and put it in a letter and told her to kiss it too.

She did so and kept it all her life. And it is still here today, over a hundred years later.

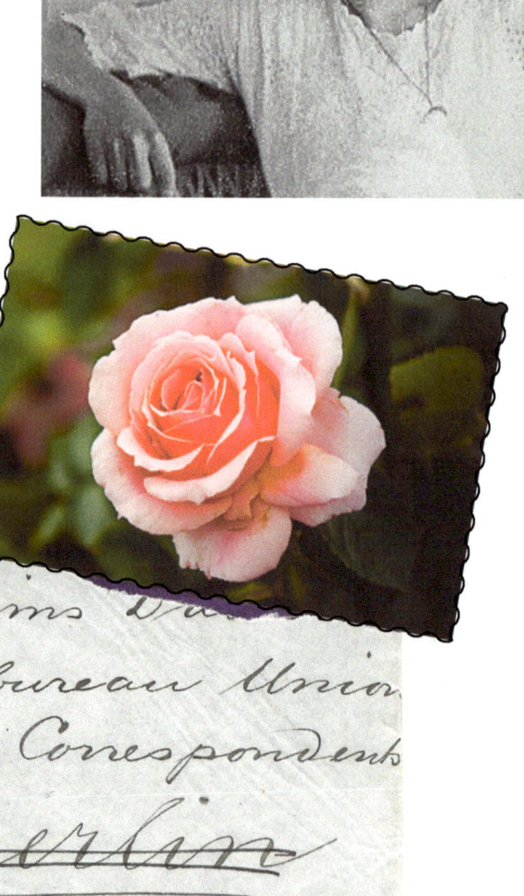

Gothenburg, 11th Aug. 09.-

Dearest-Dearest "älskling".-

Your long sweet letter to-hand yesterday, when I came out to "Särö" and you should have seen me.- I came up the veranda stairs, found the door locked, but I could see your letter on the table.- I rushed to the side door and read your letter, yes read it more

1909

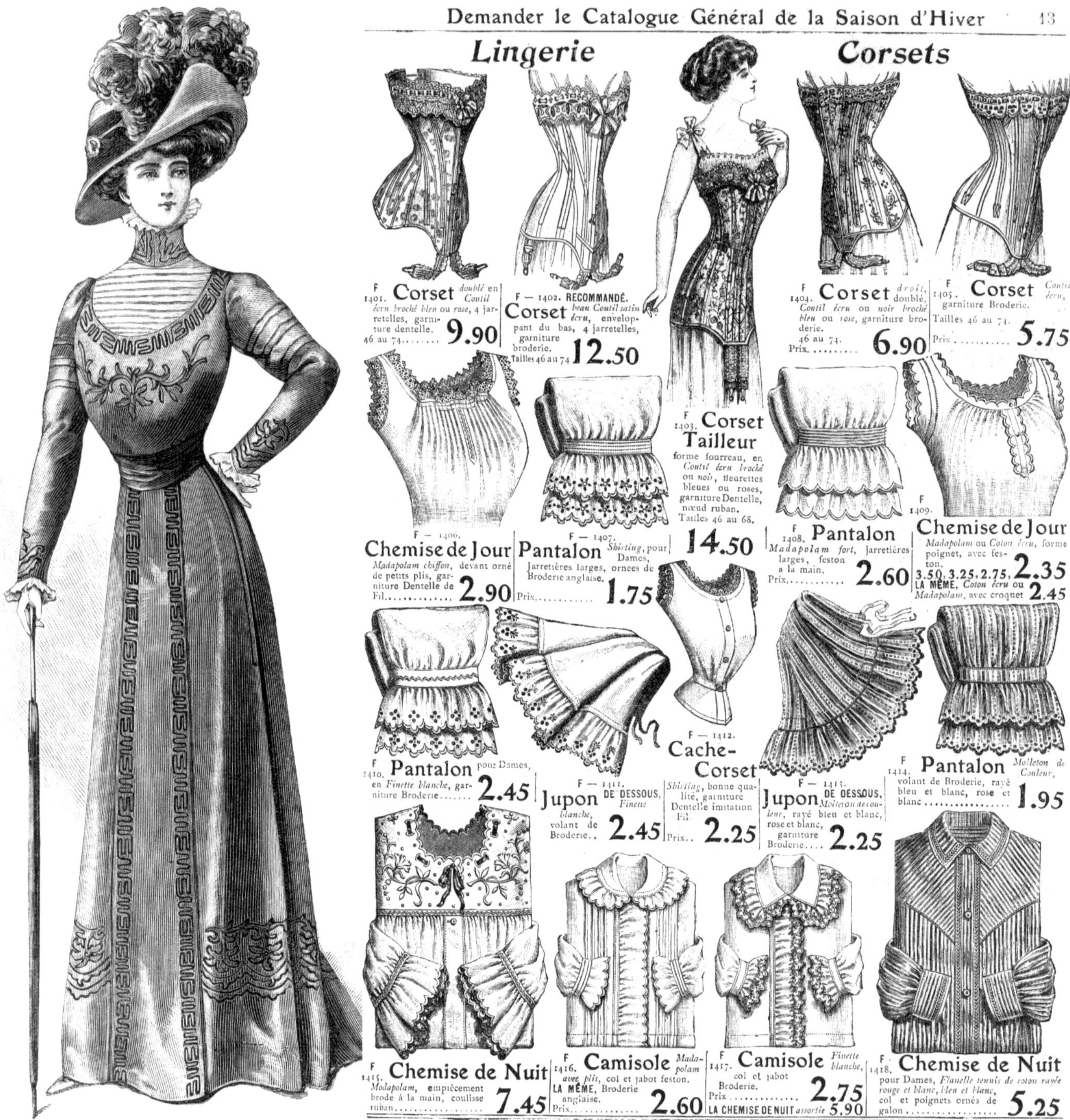

Lingerie Corsets

F 1401. **Corset** *doublé* en *Coutil écru broché bleu* ou *rose*, 4 jarretelles, garniture dentelle. 46 au 74........ **9.90**

F — 1402. RECOMMANDÉ. **Corset** *beau Coutil satin écru*, enveloppant du bas, 4 jarretelles, garniture broderie. Tailles 46 au 74 **12.50**

F 1403. **Corset Tailleur** forme fourreau, en *Coutil écru broché* ou *noir*, fleurettes bleues ou roses, garniture Dentelle, nœud ruban. Tailles 46 au 68. **14.50**

F 1404. **Corset** *droit*, doublé, *Coutil écru* ou *noir broché bleu* ou *rose*, garniture broderie. 46 au 74. Prix......... **6.90**

F 1405. **Corset** *Coutil écru*, garniture Broderie. Tailles 46 au 74. Prix.......... **5.75**

F — 1406. **Chemise de Jour** *Madapolam chiffon*, devant orné de petits plis, garniture Dentelle de Fil............ **2.90**

F — 1407. **Pantalon** *Shirting*, pour Dames, Jarretières larges, ornées de Broderie anglaise. Prix........... **1.75**

F 1408. **Pantalon** *Madapolam fort*, jarretières larges, feston à la main. Prix........... **2.60**

F 1409. **Chemise de Jour** *Madapolam* ou *Coton écru*, forme poignet, avec feston. 3.50, 3.25, 2.75, **2.35**
LA MÊME, *Coton écru* ou *Madapolam*, avec croquet **2.45**

F 1410. **Pantalon** pour Dames, en *Finette blanche*, garniture Broderie....... **2.45**

F — 1411. **Jupon** DE DESSOUS, *Finette blanche*, volant de Broderie.. **2.45**

F — 1412. **Cache-Corset** *Shirting*, bonne qualité, garniture Dentelle imitation Fil. Prix.. **2.25**

F — 1413. **Jupon** DE DESSOUS, *Molleton de couleur*, rayé bleu et blanc, rose et blanc, garniture Broderie.... **2.25**

F 1414. **Pantalon** *Molleton de Couleur*, volant de Broderie, rayé bleu et blanc, rose et blanc................. **1.95**

F 1415. **Chemise de Nuit** *Madapolam*, empiècement brodé à la main, coulisse ruban................. **7.45**

F 1416. **Camisole** *Madapolam avec plis*, col et jabot feston. LA MÊME, Broderie anglaise. Prix............ **2.60**

F 1417. **Camisole** *Finette blanche*, col et jabot Broderie. Prix.............. **2.75**
LA CHEMISE DE NUIT *assortie* **5.90**

F 1418. **Chemise de Nuit** pour Dames, *Flanelle tennis de coton rayée rouge et blanc, bleu et blanc*, col et poignets ornés de galon................. **5.25**

OLGA ASSEMBLES HER TROUSSEAU

(THE CLOTHES AND PERSONAL POSSESSIONS THAT A WOMAN COLLECTS WHEN SHE IS ABOUT TO GET MARRIED)

" I've nearly compiled my underwear and will now begin on hats, dresses and coats. I prefer quality over quantity..."

Miss Olga Dawson, August 17, 1909

Olga and her family spent the two months before the wedding in Paris, to travel in Germany and to buy her trousseau. She had been given a thousand dollars by her father for this purpose.

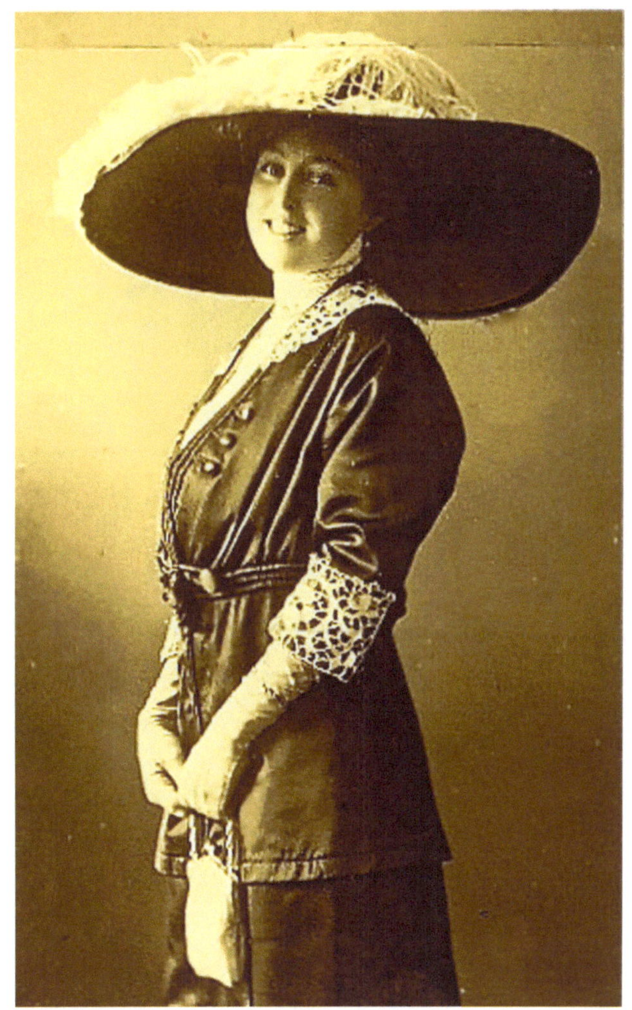

Left:
Paris fashion 1909.
Olga confessed that she had a liking for lace underwear, but Folke wrote to her that she also needed something warm for Swedish winters.

Right:
Olga sent this photo from Germany. Folke wrote he hardly recognized her under the big hat.

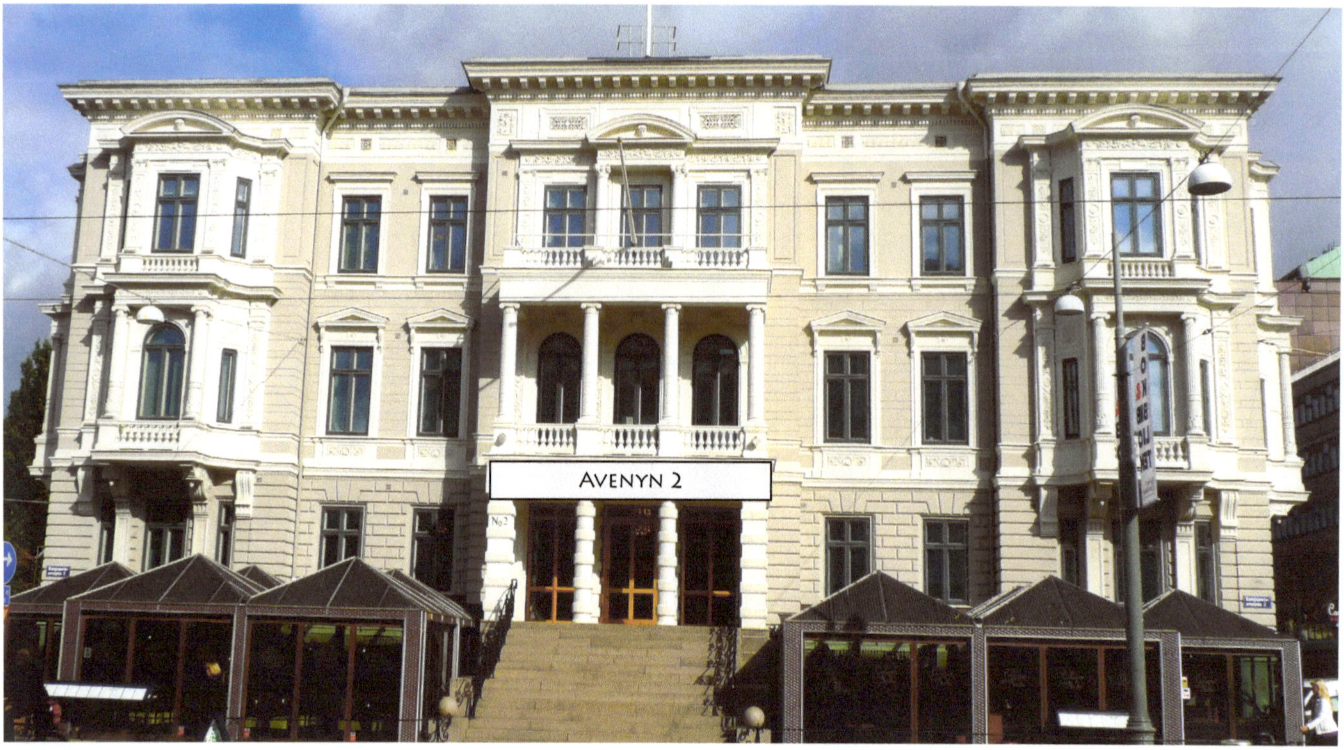

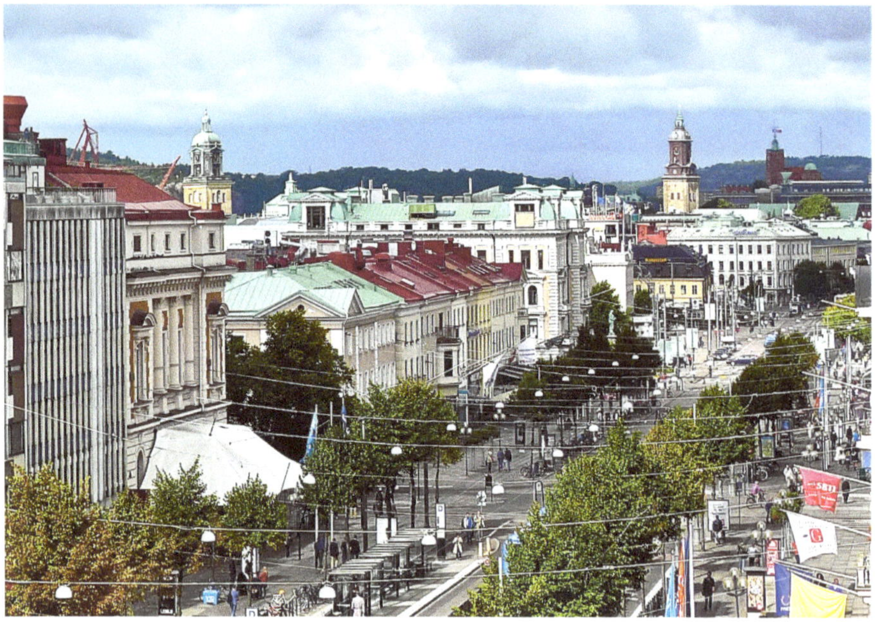

Folke grew up in this building on Avenyn 2, in Gothenburg. The building today, looks pretty much as it did in 1909 except for the front garden which is gone.

Grandmother Olga told me that in those days, it would take forever to walk up or down Avenyn, (the main street) because she would meet so many friends and relatives, and she ended up talking with all of them.

Avenyn today (left).

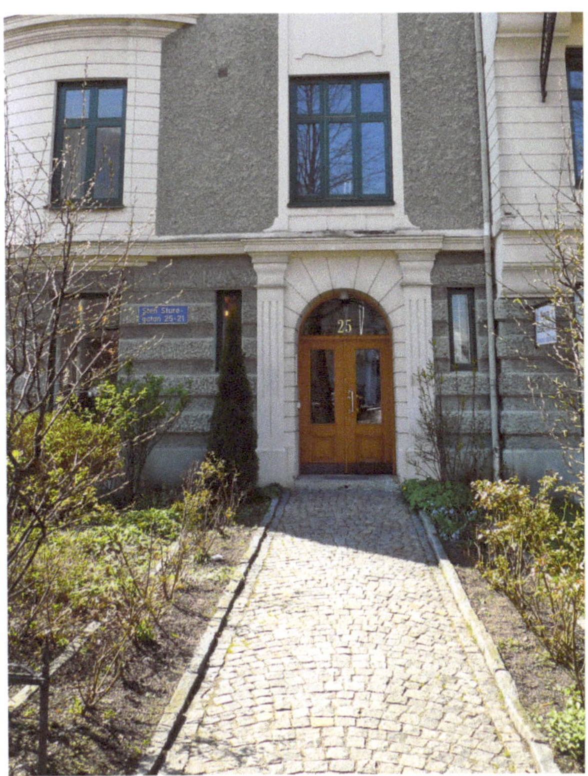

THE FIRST HOME

Not far away from where Folke grew up (left), Olga and Folke arranged for their first home. This was done after they were engaged during the summer of 1909. They did not have much time for buying furniture and it was all done in an hour.

While Olga was travelling in Germany and preparing for the wedding in Paris, Folke took care of much of the furnishing of the flat. In his letters to Olga he tells her what he has done and looks forward to the day they can both move in.

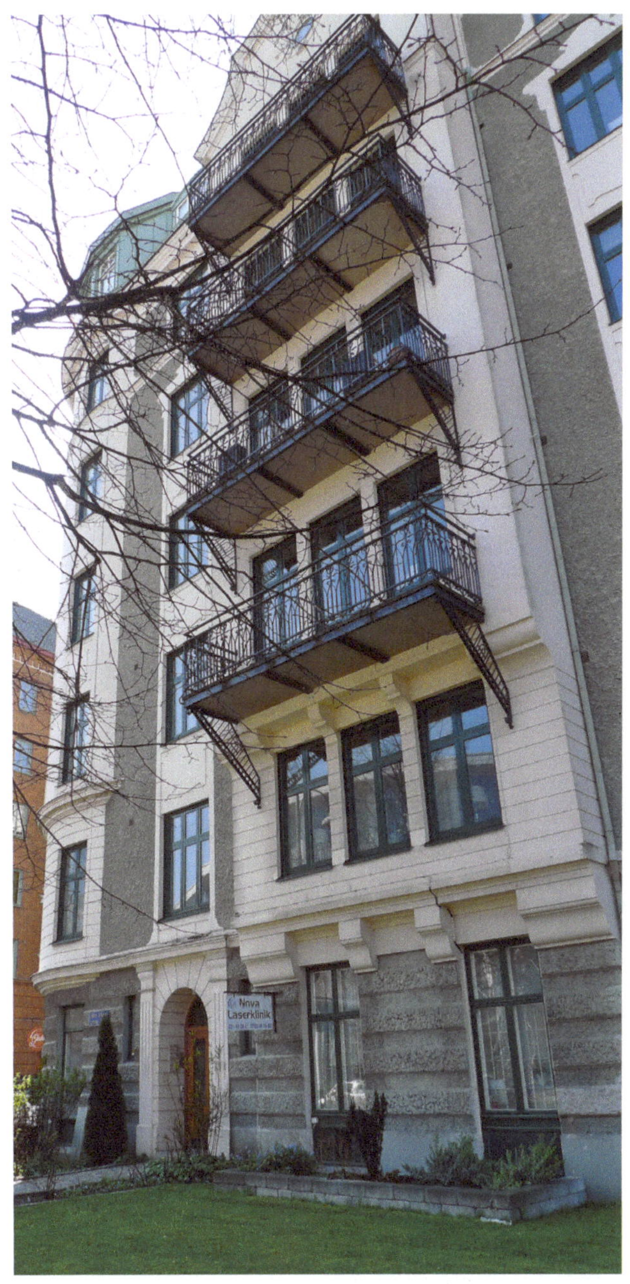

STEN STUREGATAN 25

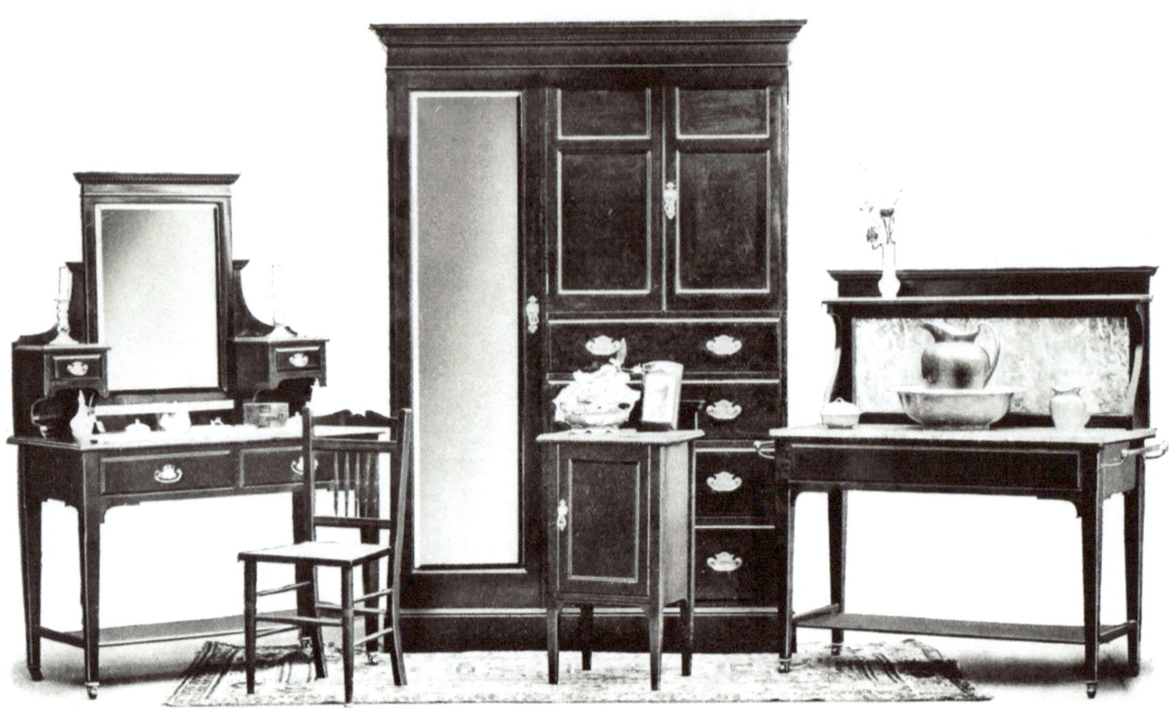

In 1909, the young Olga and Folke were in a hurry to furnish their new flat and did what people often did in those days, they bought "suites" of furniture such as this bedroom suite from London's Maple and Co. From Folke's letters, we know that the couple had chosen a living room suite in leather.

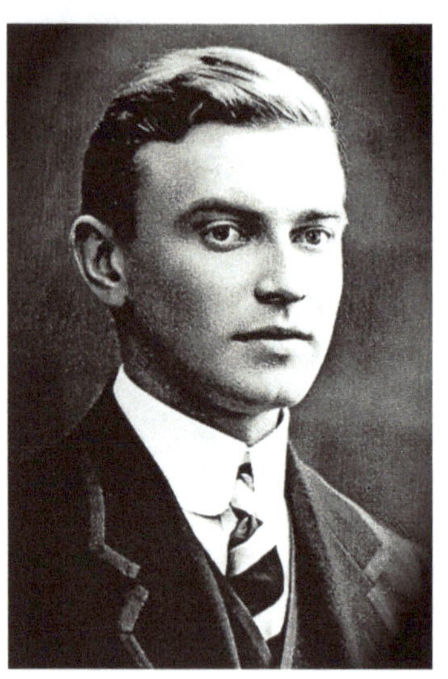

WHAT DID FOLKE EMBROIDER FOR OLGA?

In September 1909, Folke writes to Olga that he has started to embroider something for her. It keeps him busy in the evenings. It will be a surprise for Olga when they come back from the honeymoon -- for the bedroom, he wrote. A pillow perhaps?

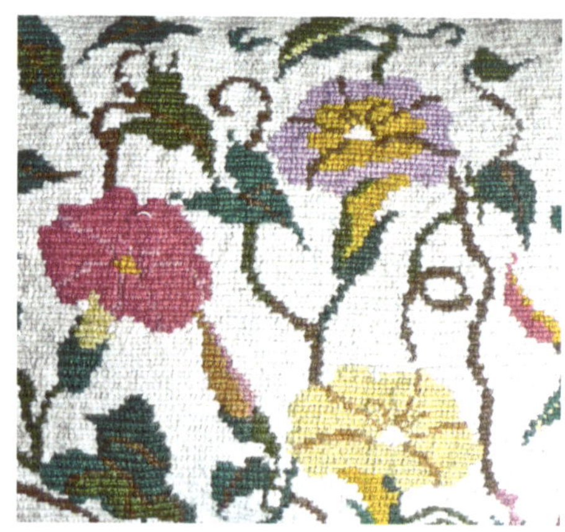

FURNISHING THE NEW HOME

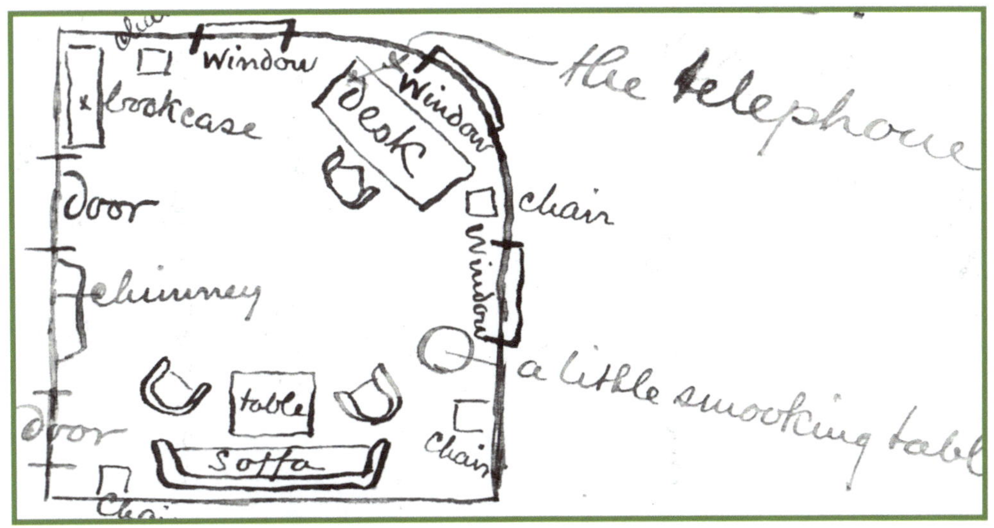

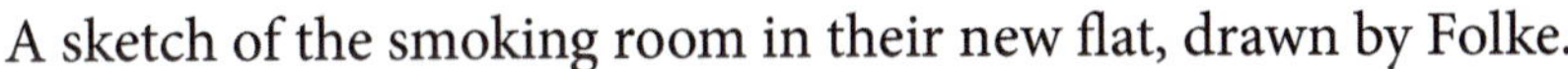
A sketch of the smoking room in their new flat, drawn by Folke.

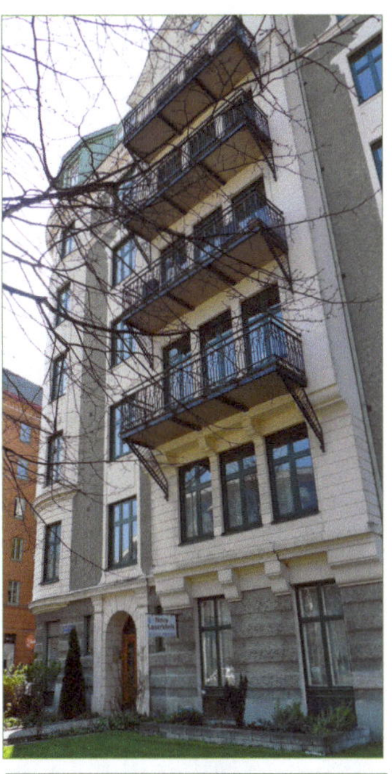

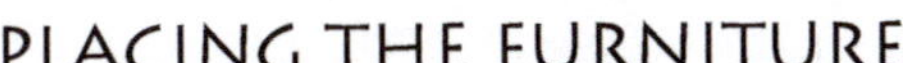
PLACING THE FURNITURE

Folke was eager to have the flat finished for their return from their honeymoon. They had earlier picked out some furniture together, but there was so much more.

Olga has seen some interesting chandeliers in Germany and Folke has ideas how to furnish their smoking room (sketch above). And where should they place their telephone? They send drawings back and forth between Germany and Sweden.

Right: A sketch of a chandelier Folke had seen and he was very keen to share it with Olga. They wisely decide to buy the chandeliers together when they come back from the wedding. But there are many more things to be arranged before Folke leaves for Paris -- silver, glasses, custom made bed sheets etc.

Folke's father Axel, is both helpful and generous when it comes to the rugs and curtains.

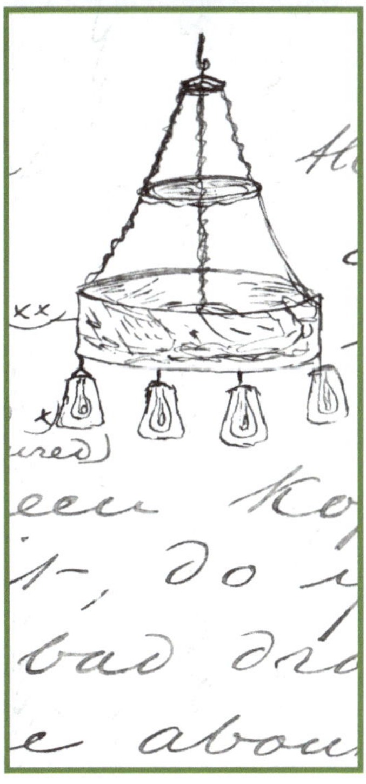

FOLKE SHOULD WORK, BUT...

In August 1909, two months before Folke was to be married, a general strike broke out and all of Sweden was paralyzed. The company sawmill could no longer produce the laths or pit props to sell to Britain. For many weeks, there was no work for Folke and his father. This national strike of 1909 was a great loss for the Swedish workers who really had not planned it at all, but were forced into it through the "lockout" by their employers. They eventually had to accept a cut in pay as their unions were weak and did not have funds to hold out for a long time. The unions received financial help from abroad, but it was not enough.

Folke's love-letters to Olga also describe how the strike developed and how it affected the life of the family -- and how the strike eventually ended. Gothenburg at this time had a great number of factories, and the textile industry was very large. The mill owners were concerned about sabotage and fires and had guards posted.

If a factory burned during the strike, the ordinary insurance did not pay for the damage if it was sabotage. Owners resorted to extremely expensive insurance from abroad.

(Read more in **MY DARLING OLGA Folke Jonsson Letters 1909-1961, Leif Södergren)**

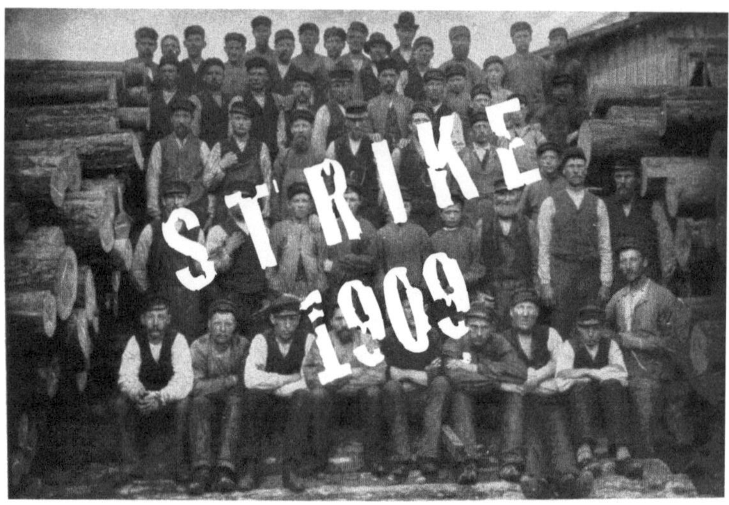

At the company saw mill, all the workers were on strike as were all workers in Sweden.

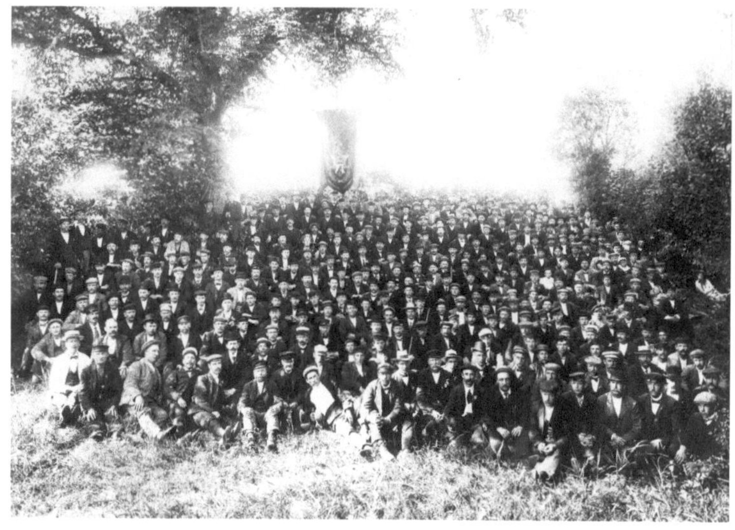

Paper workers locked out in Skutskär -- for not accepting lowered wages. (Folkrörelsearkivet för Uppsala län)

THE FAMILY BUSINESS
JONSSON, STERNHAGEN & CO., AB
FOUNDED 1872
GOTHENBURG SWEDEN

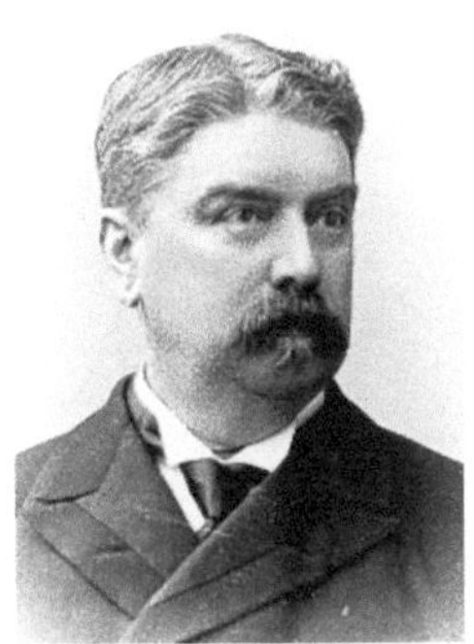

JONSSON, STERNHAGEN & CO., was a large export company founded by Folke's father, Axel Jonsson, and a partner Harald Sternhagen.
The company was very successful selling timber in the form of "laths" (as in lath and plaster) used for building houses and pit props used to in coal mines -- Britain was in great need of these products, being at the height of its empire. A lot of new building was going on in Victorian England, supplying housing for the expanding middle class.

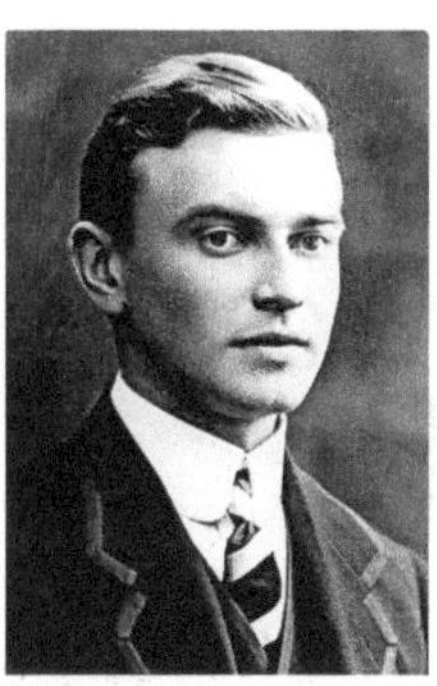

LATHS
A large export product was "laths". They were used in those days, as plasterboard is used today, for interior walls and ceilings. Thin strips (laths) were nailed on wall or ceiling studs, with a space between, and the plaster was applied.

Axel Jonsson travelled extensively in Britain to introduce the "Swedish lath" which was of excellent quality and cheaper to produce. Jonsson Sternhagen had a virtual monopoly.

PIT PROPS (right)
Pit props held up the walls in British coal mines and were also a large export product.

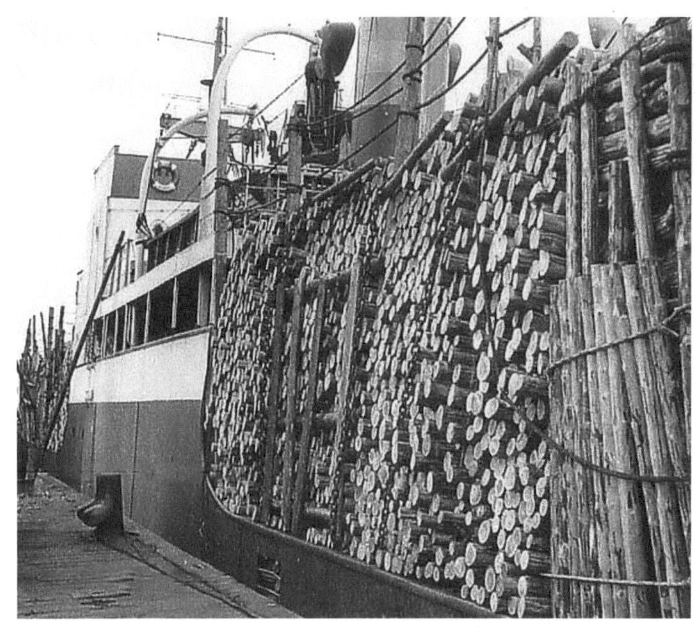

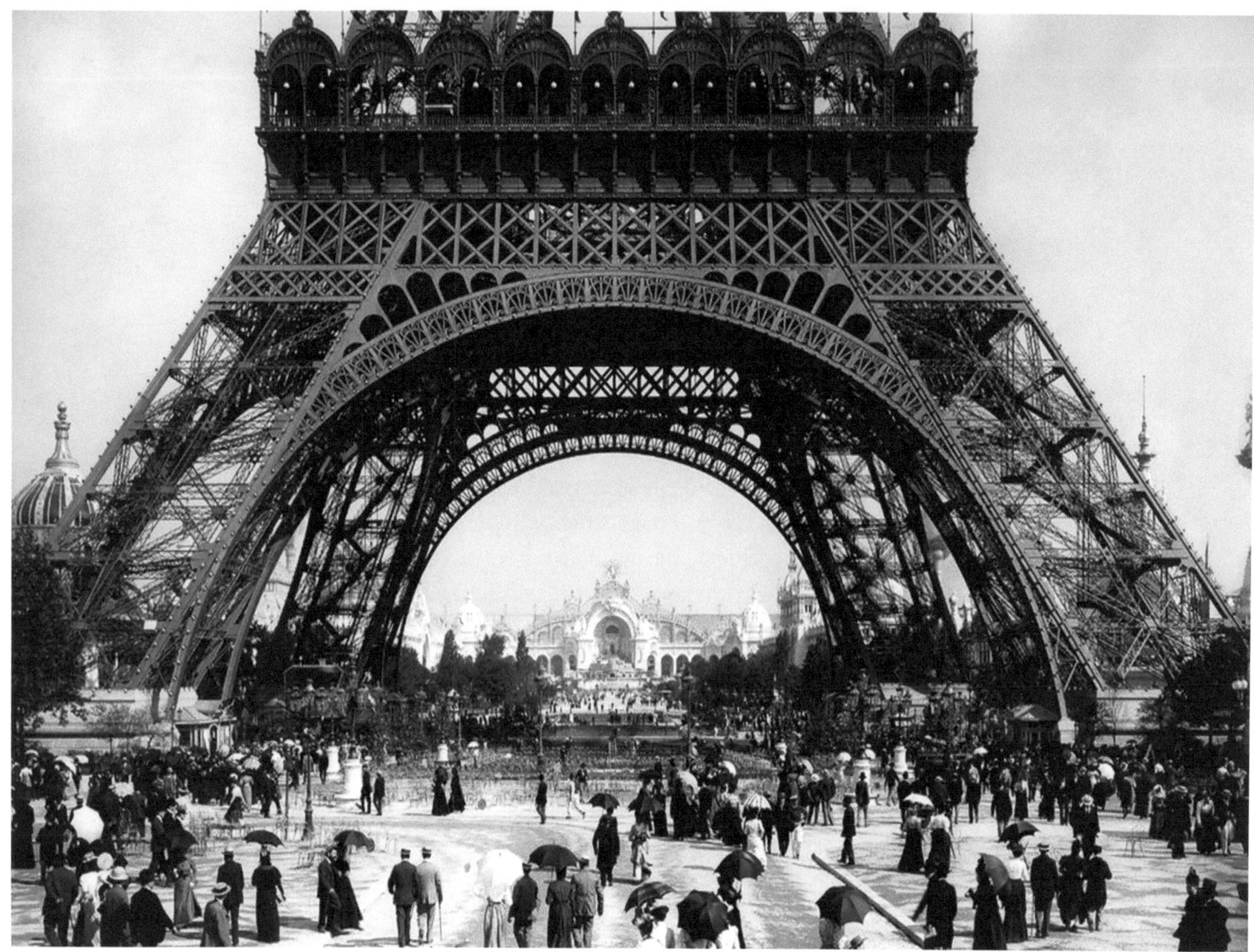

Folke proposed to Olga on top of the Eiffel Tower. They had many happy memories from Paris and decided to marry there. But it was easier said than done.

If two foreigners wished to marry in Paris, one of them had to show proof of a 30 day residency in the city. That responsibility fell to Olga who travelled from Brussels to Paris. Olga travelled unchaperoned, and found it quite thrilling to arrive alone at the large railway station, Gare du Nord in Paris.

She sent Folke a long list of certificates that must be translated into French, and sent, but there was more to comply with...

(More in **MY DARLING OLGA Folke Jonsson Letters 1909-1961)**

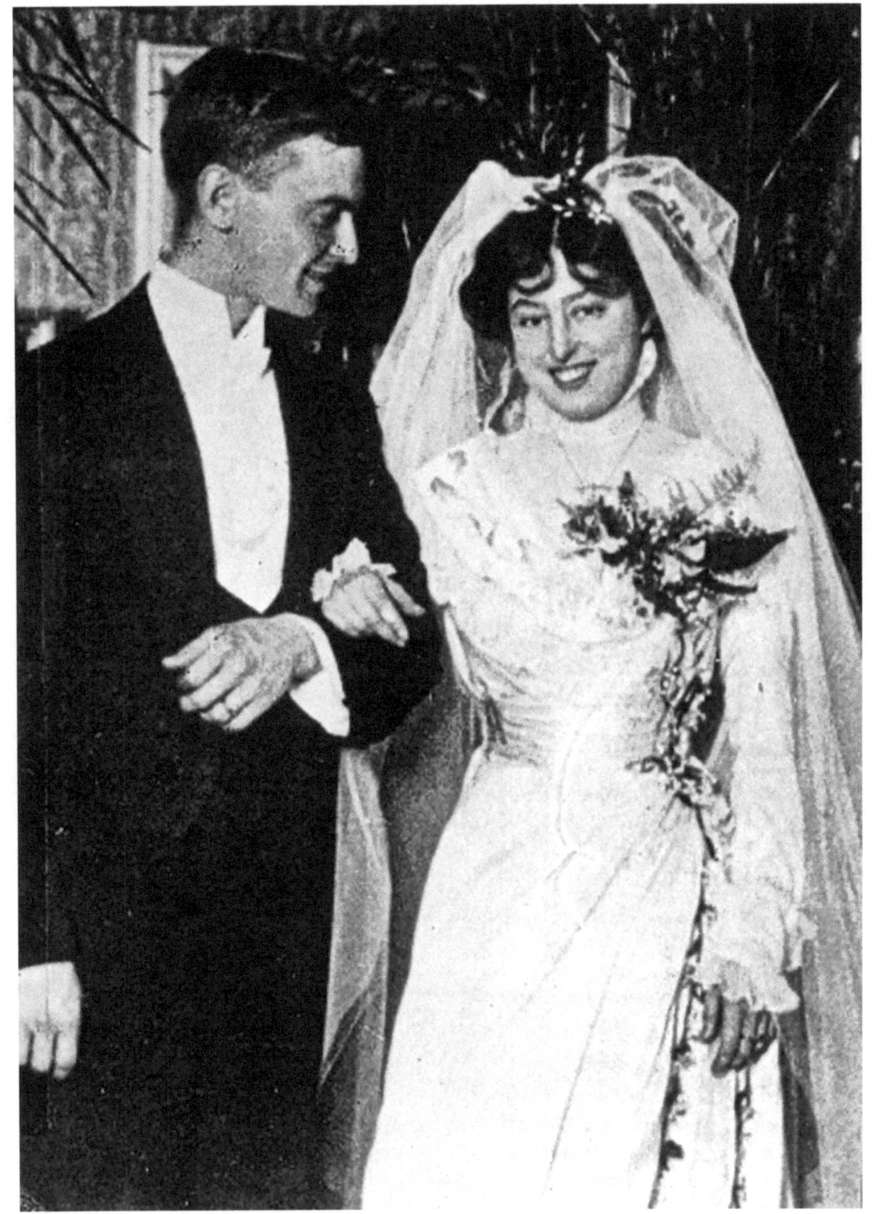

PARIS
October 18, 1909

OLGA AND HER CHILDREN ON A JOURNEY TO FLORIDA

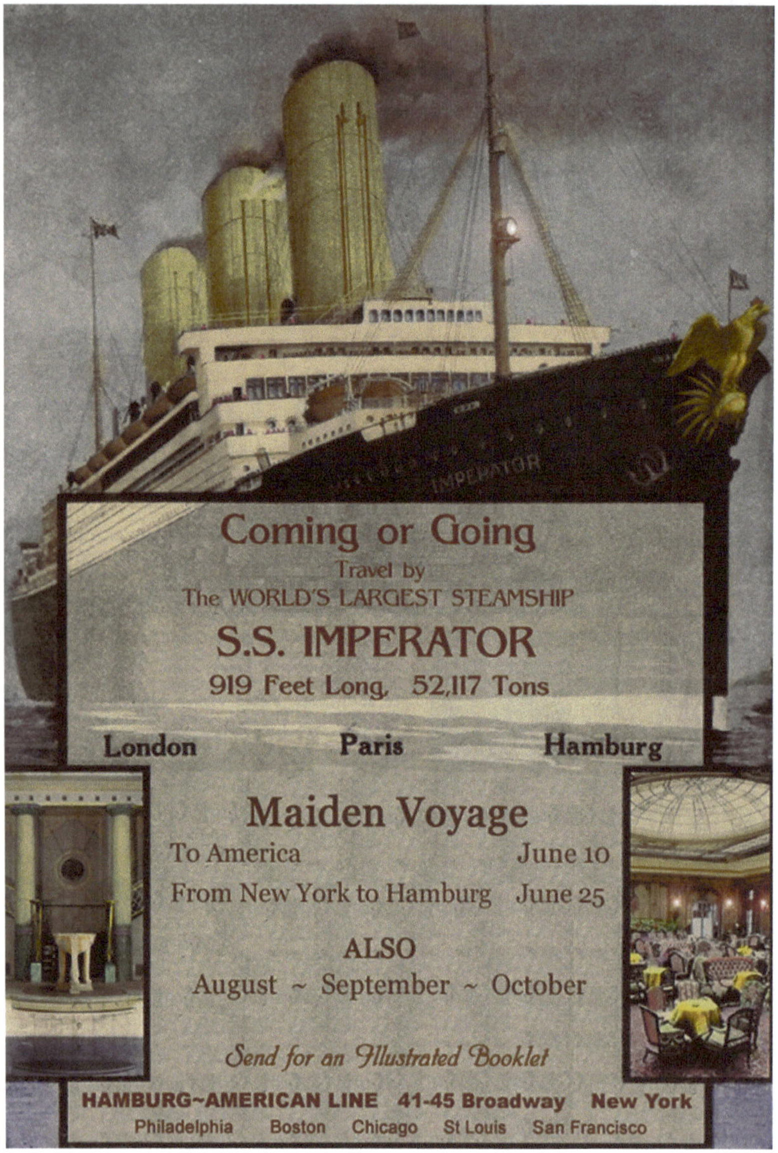

Coming or Going

Travel by

The WORLD'S LARGEST STEAMSHIP

S.S. IMPERATOR

919 Feet Long, 52,117 Tons

London Paris Hamburg

Maiden Voyage

To America June 10

From New York to Hamburg June 25

ALSO

August ~ September ~ October

Send for an Illustrated Booklet

HAMBURG~AMERICAN LINE 41-45 Broadway New York

Philadelphia Boston Chicago St Louis San Francisco

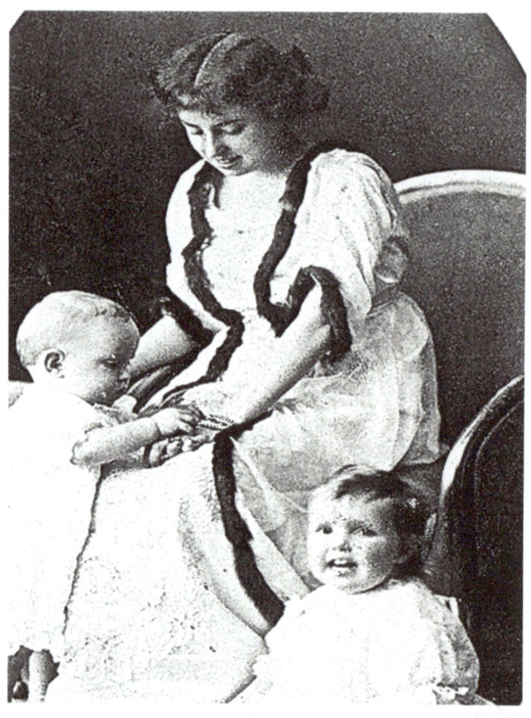

In September 1913, Folke's wife, Olga, their two children, Anita, three, and Billy, two, and the nanny Ida, set out on a journey to Jacksonville Florida where they would visit Olga's parents.

They went by train to Hamburg where they boarded the S.S Imperator which was the biggest and most luxurious passenger ship in the world. On board, a large, full-figure painting of the German emperor proudly dominated the majestic staircase.

WILL OLGA RETURN FOR CHRISTMAS?

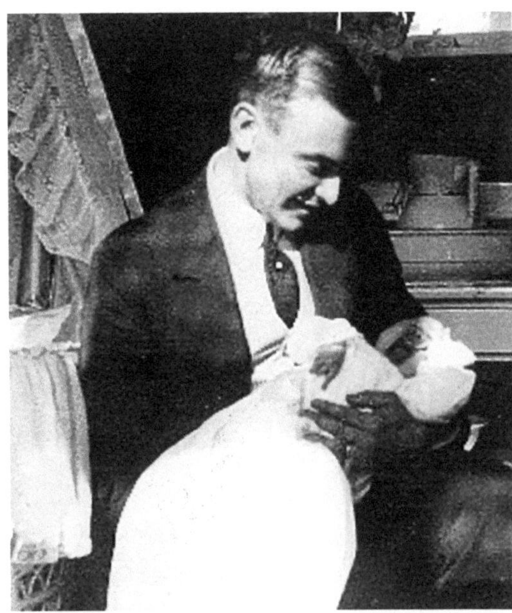

The four month old Mary Carita stayed behind with Folke, looked after by a nurse. But Folke did not realize how painful the separation would be. He was heartbroken and wrote a letter almost every other day, pleading with Olga to come home.

Olga had said that she intended to come back before Christmas and Folke sincerely hoped that she would stick to what he perceived as a promise. But...

(Read more in **MY DARLING OLGA** Folke Jonsson Letters 1909-1962)

1.

Gothenburg, 22nd Nov. 1913.

My own dearest darling.—

Thanks sweetheart for your letter of 9th inst. which I received this morning.— You do not know how happy your letters do me.— I only wished that you will soon be home. You say darling be a man, but you wouldn't say that again if you knew how hard and sad it is for me to be alone here, day after day.— By now I suppose

A NEW HOME

Folke had selected a barren peninsula on Särö for their house-to-be. It was not where most of the posh people lived, in the very heart of the fashionable seaside resort, Särö, on the Swedish West coast.

The peninsula Folke had chosen would provide a grand, more secluded and spacious setting for Olga and Folke's new home.

Olga was shocked when she first saw what Folke proposed for their new home, on bare rock on a peninsula. Could one really build a house there? But Folke's enthusiasm was catching and when the house was finished in 1918, it had many wide terraces built from local river stones, all filled with soil and planted with trees. Very soon this barren peninsula would be green indeed.

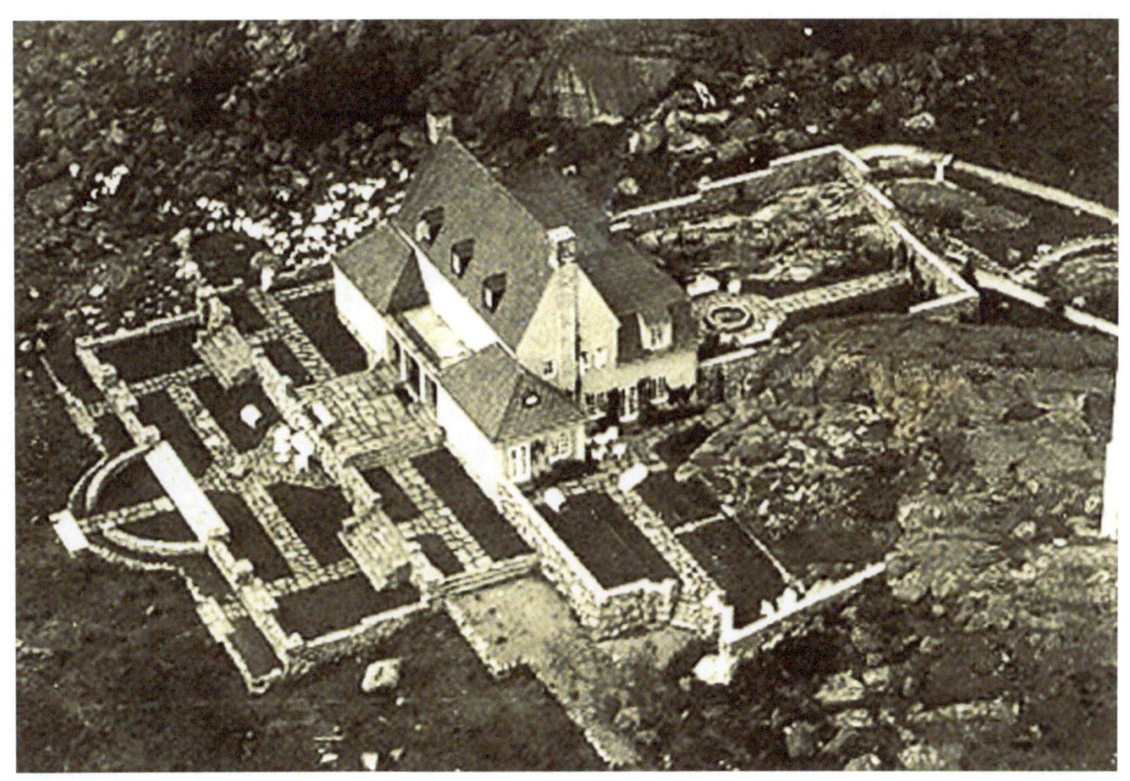

1918
LYSHOLMEN

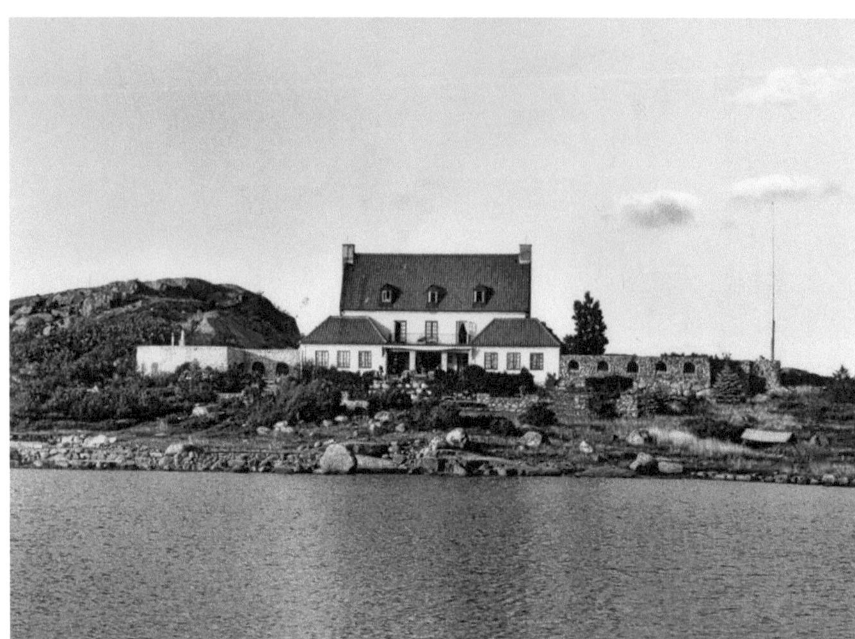

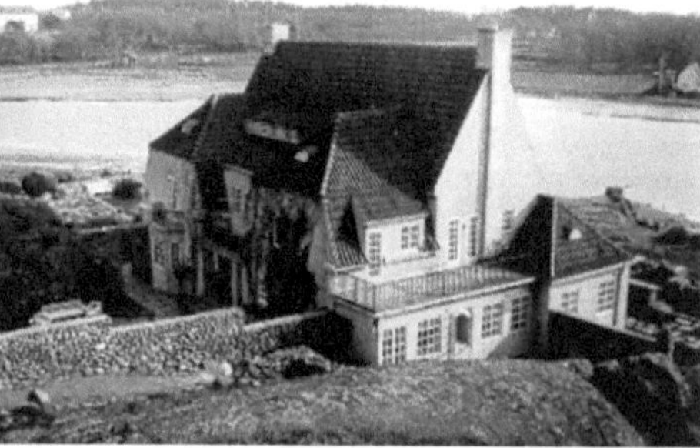

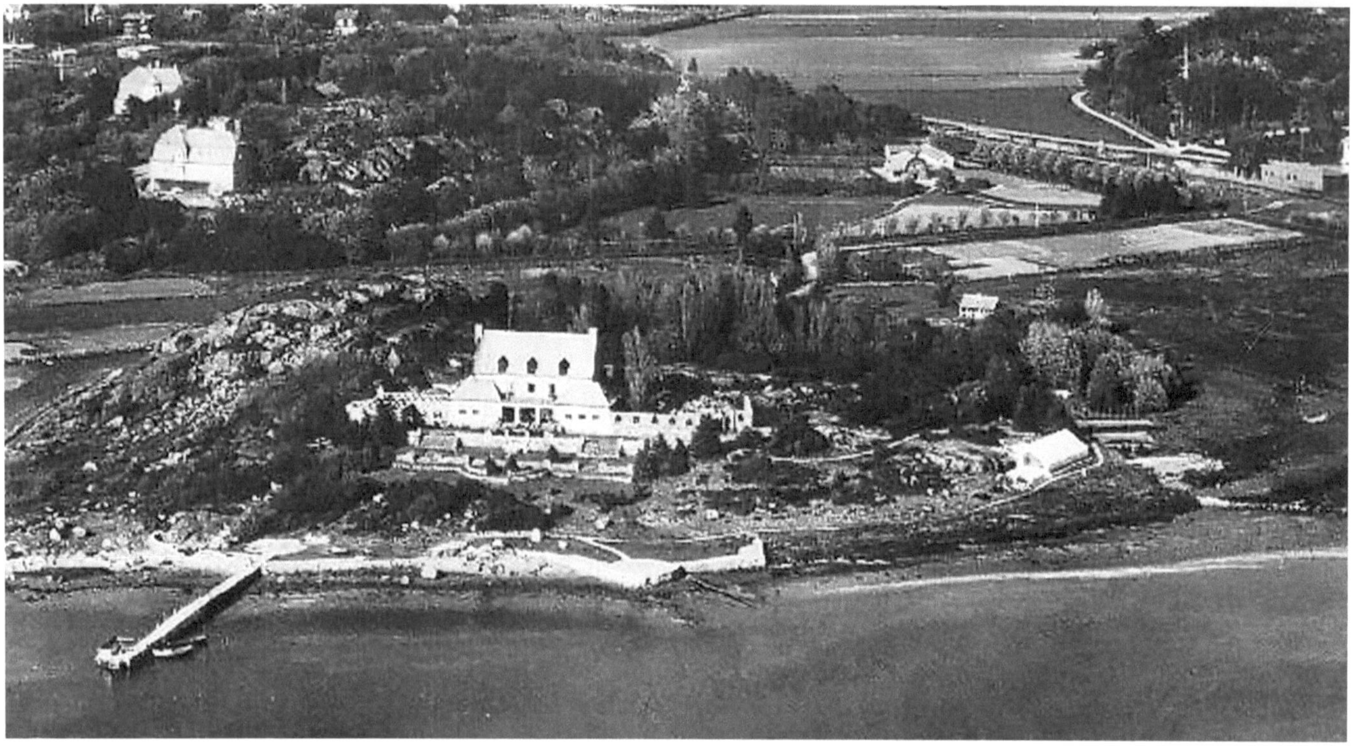

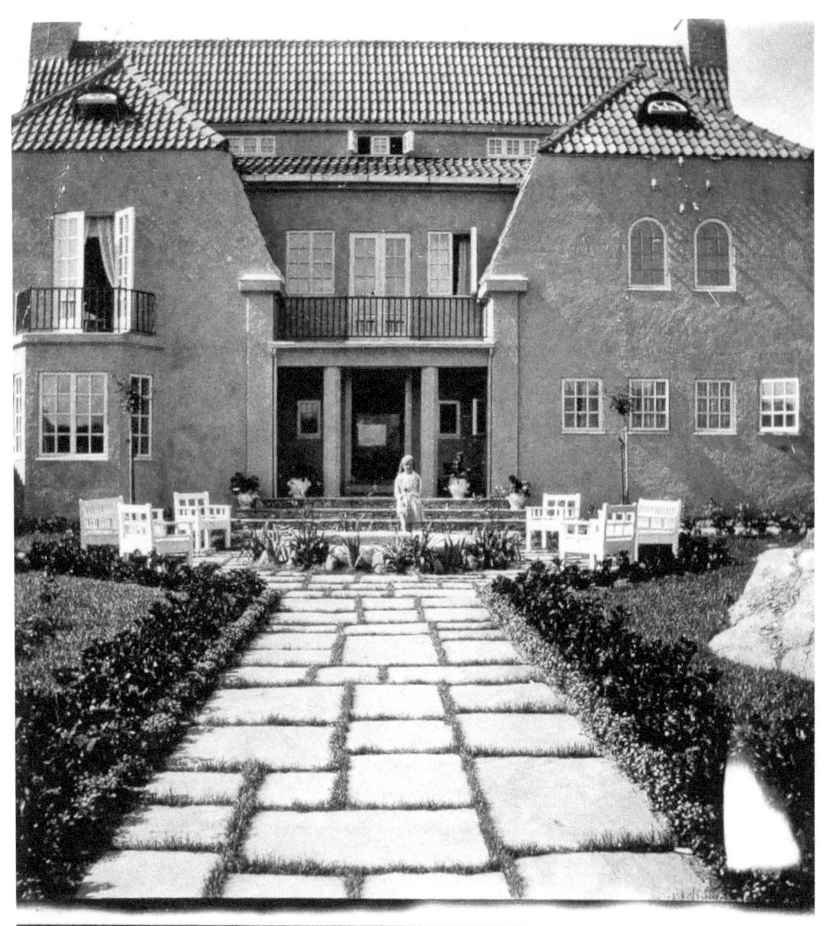

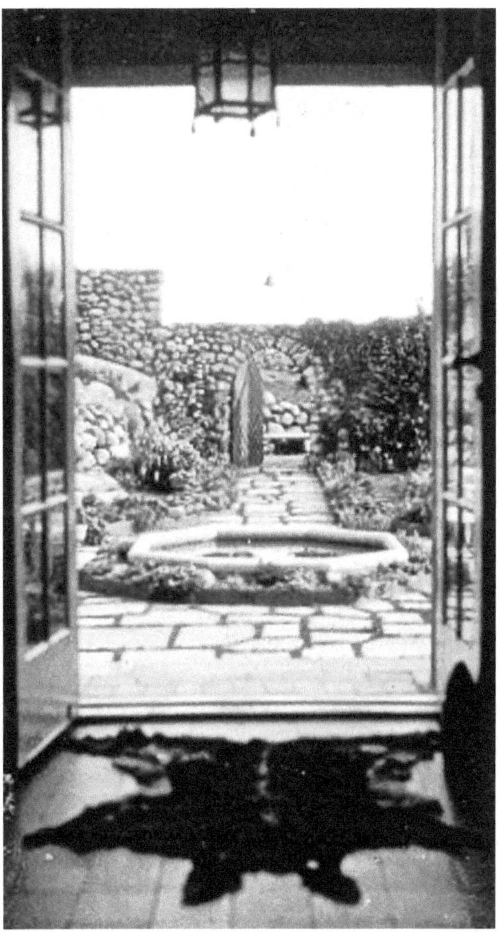

ALWAYS OPEN HOUSE AT LYSHOLMEN

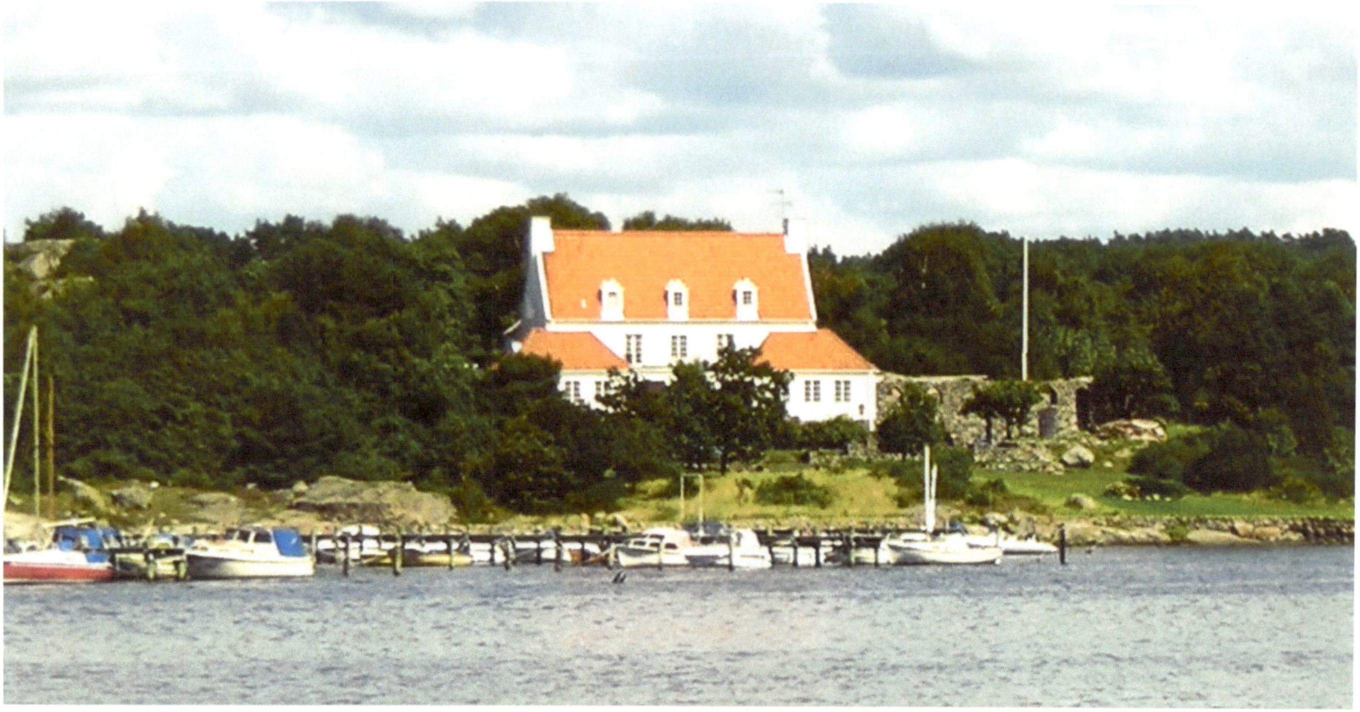

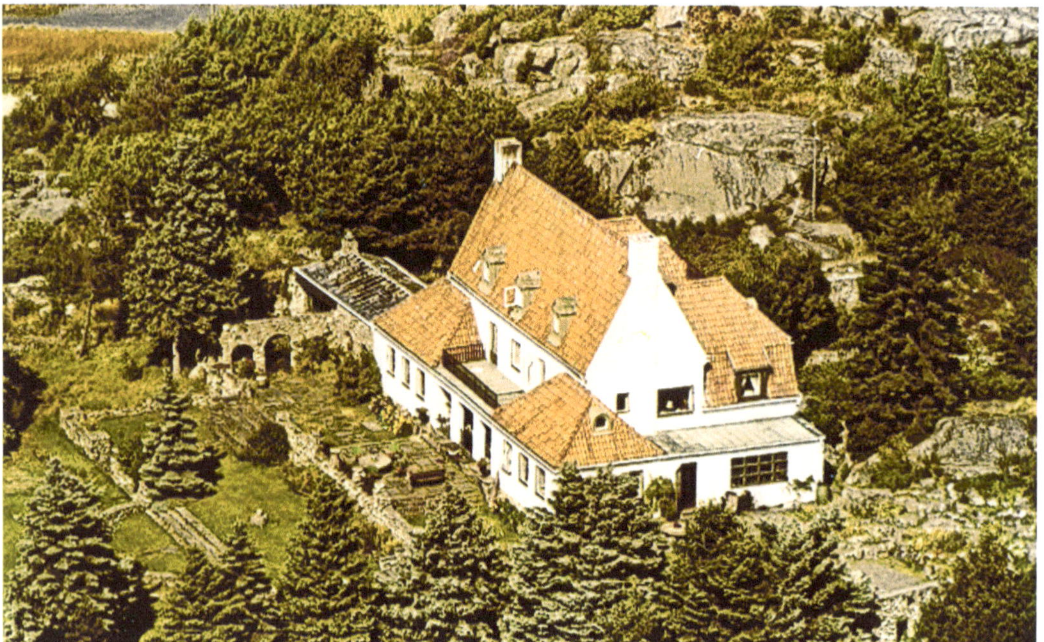

This impressive three story house on the ocean was to remain the residence for the rest of Olga and Folke's lives. It was the perfect home for the couple and their nine children.

The Winter Garden (Stengården) was an addition built on to the dining room in 1934 to create a large place for their daughter Anita's wedding (and daughter Sonja's wedding in 1935). It had a proper roof, flooring and heating (below right) Later it was turned into a "Winter Garden", with a glass roof and plants, like a large conservatory.

In the Spring, large pots of trees and plants were taken from the basement where they had been kept safe from the frost during the winter months.

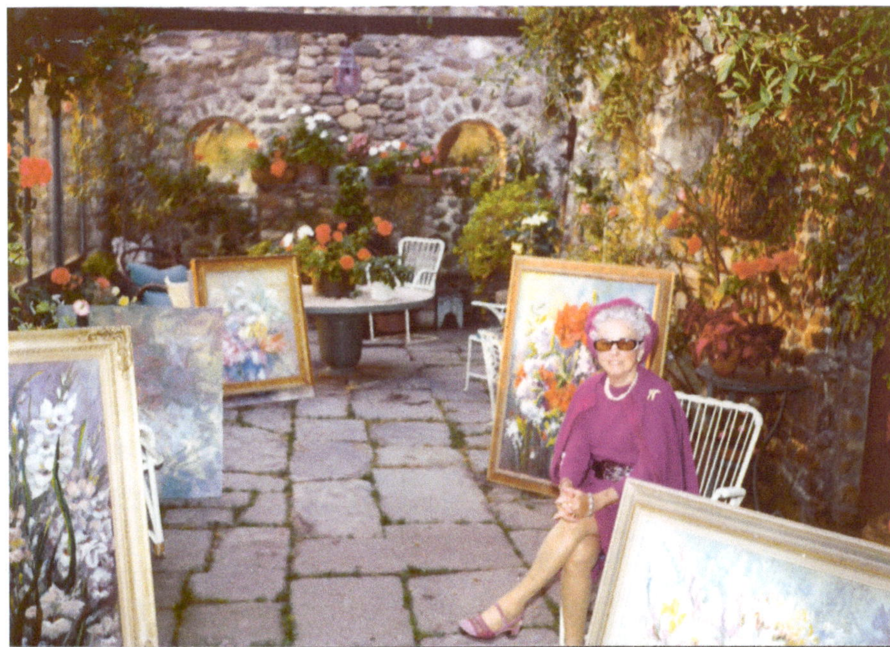

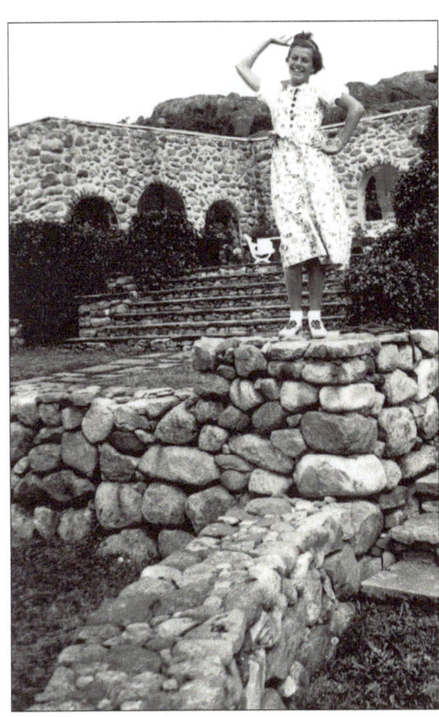

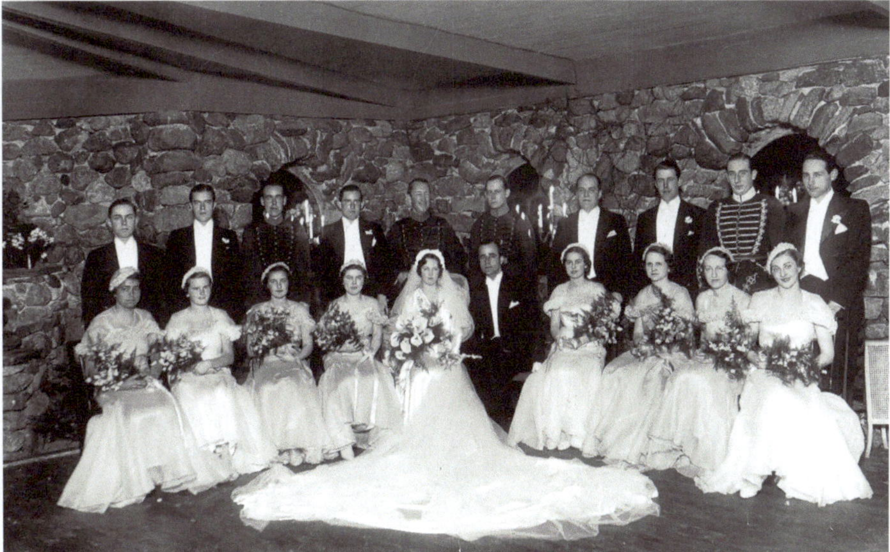

Left: In this picture from 1937, we see how the room looked from the outside, before it was reduced in size and turned into the winter garden. Also note the massive stone steps and walls that surrounded Lysholmen.

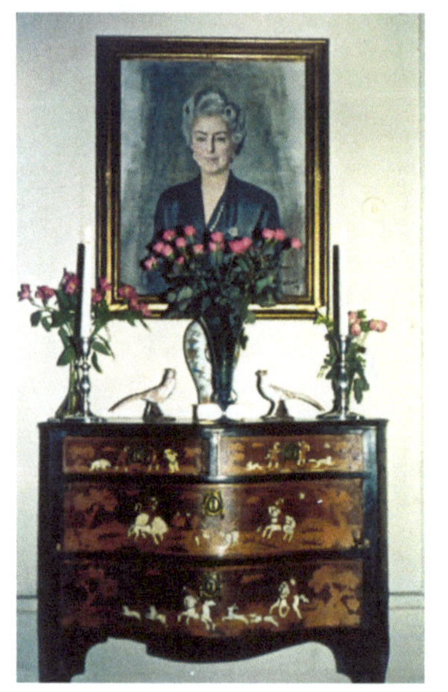

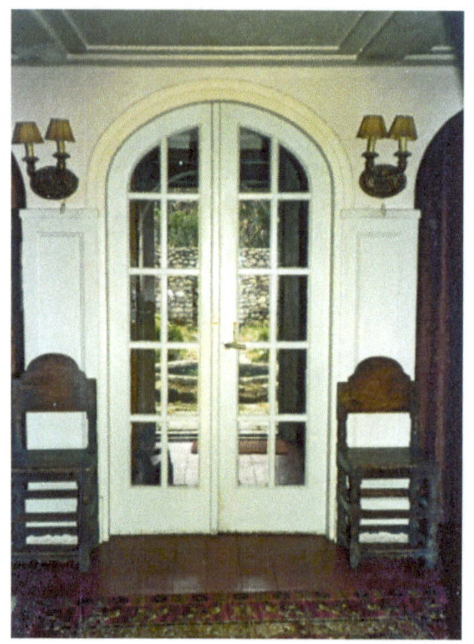

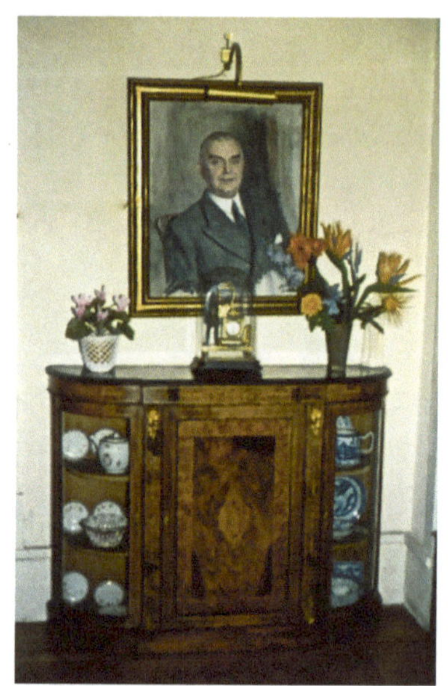

DOWNSTAIRS HALLWAY

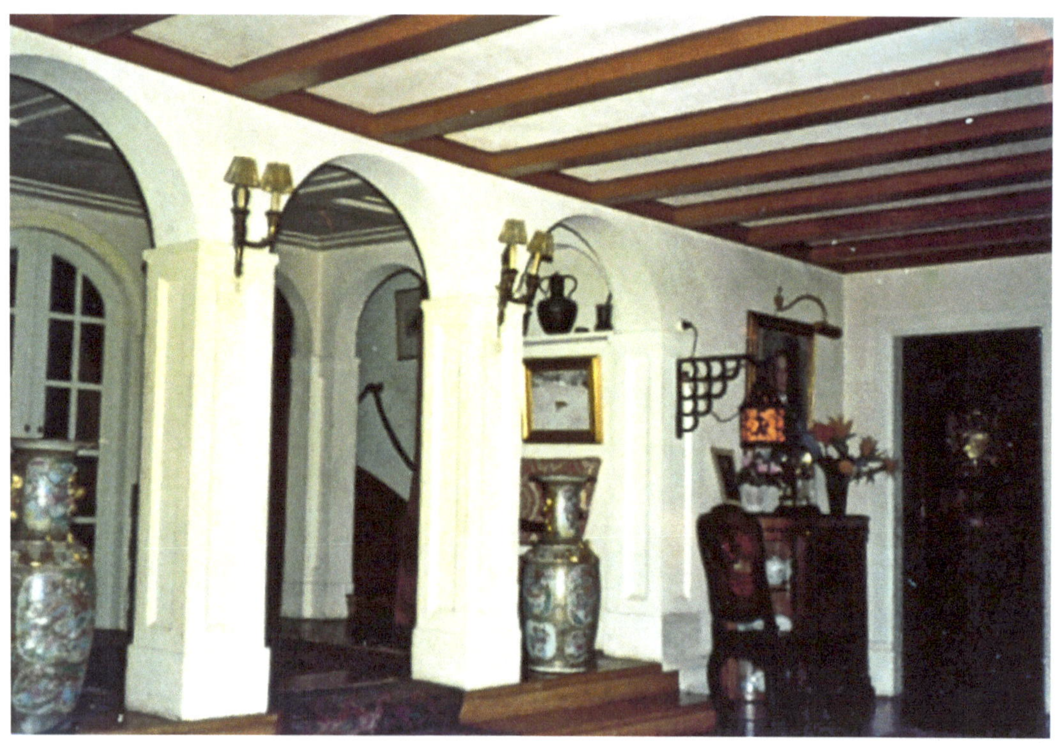

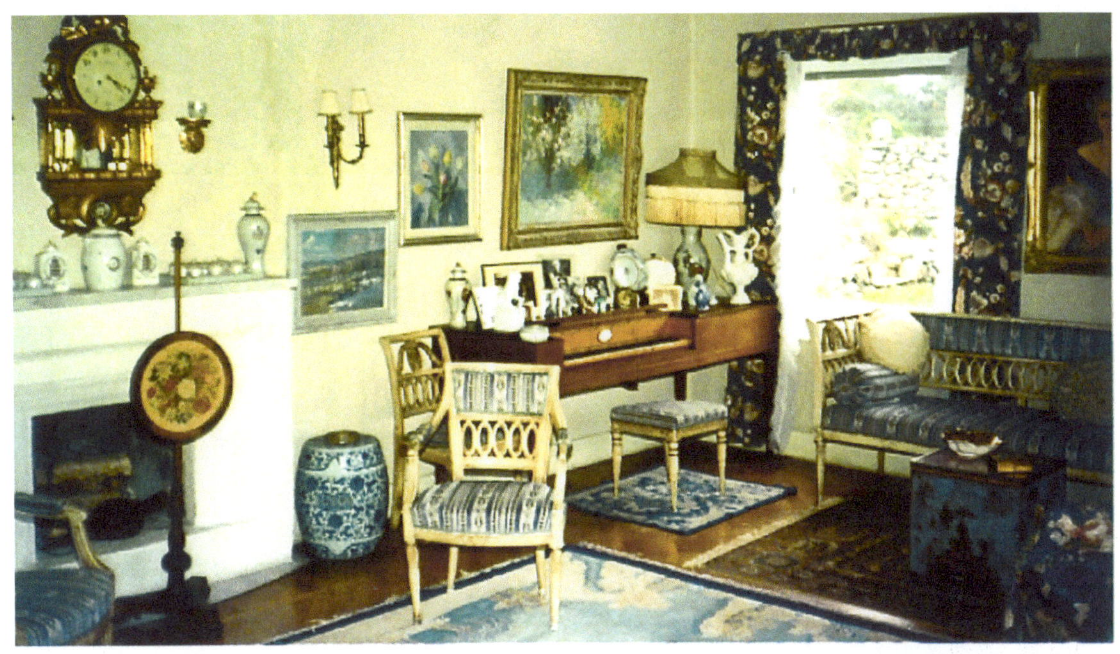

THE DAY ROOM

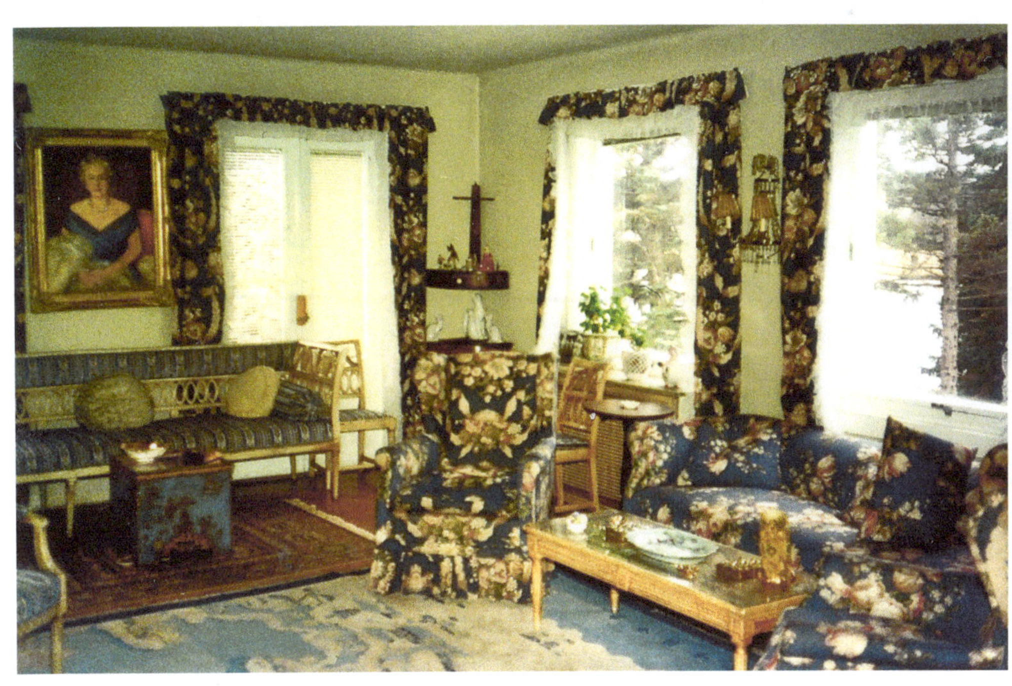

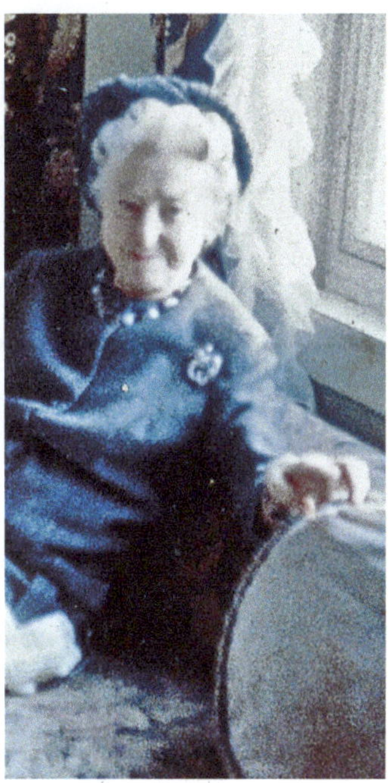

THE DINING ROOM

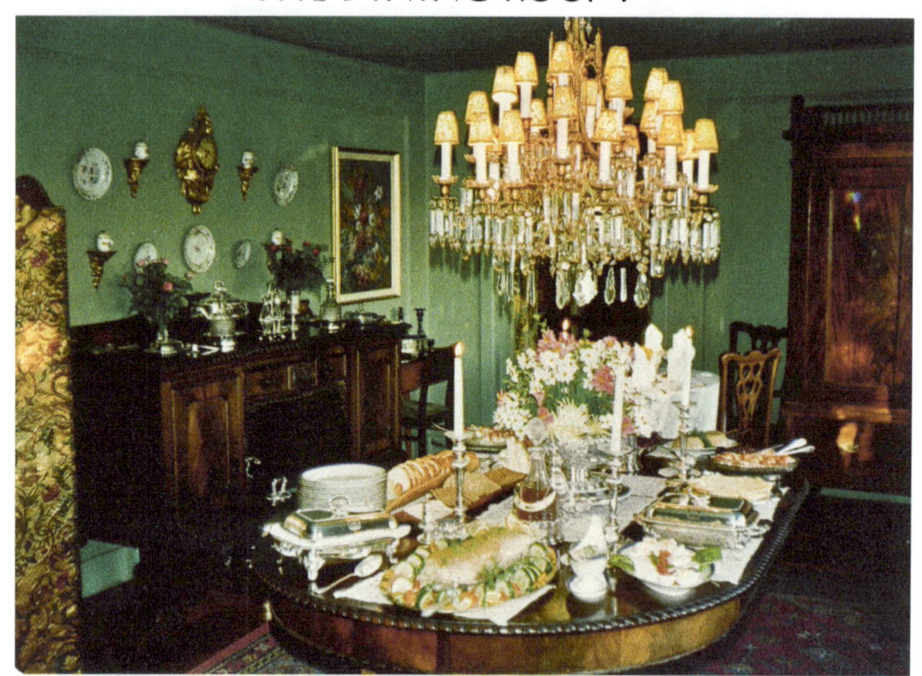

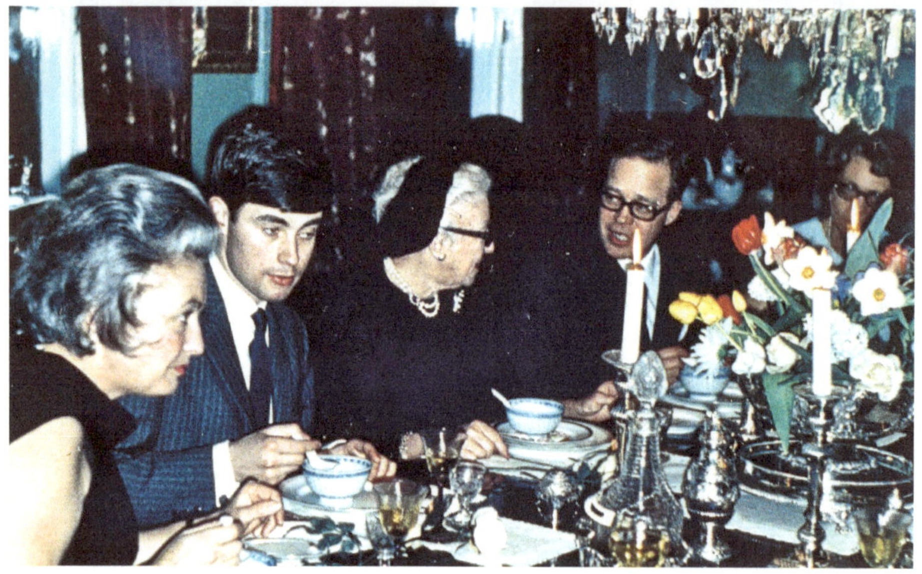

From left: Gunilla Hellström, Leif Södergren, Olga, Ulf Hellström and Maj Atterbom.

THE LIVING ROOM

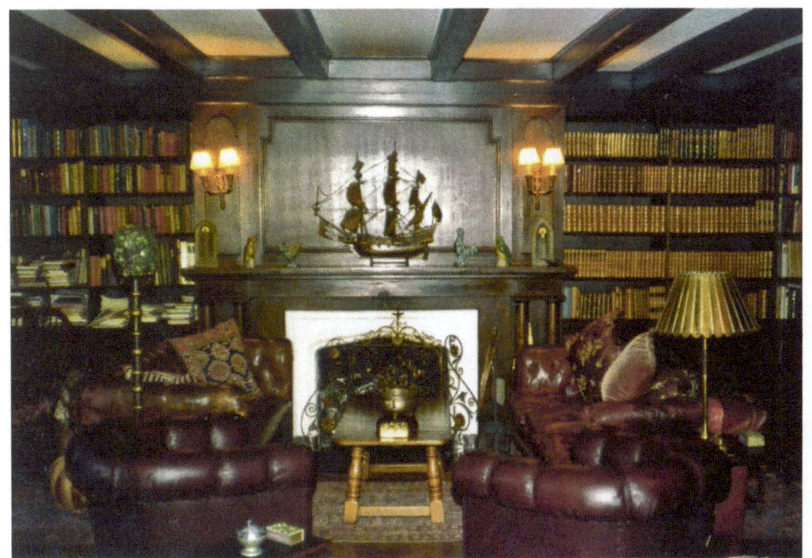

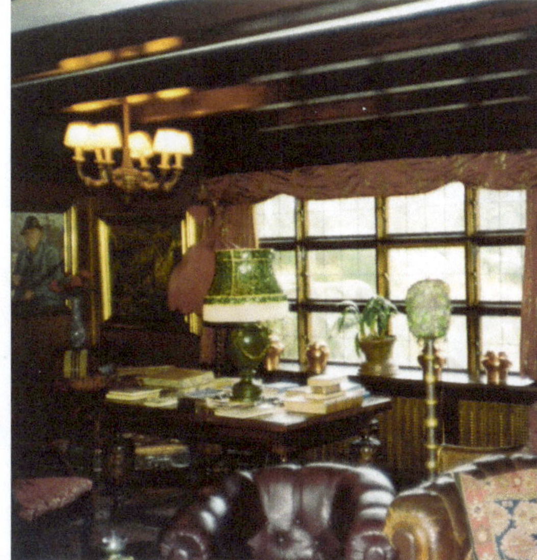

The living room was once a billiard room. It was converted to a Tudor style living room around 1930. The furniture, in oak and medieval style, was made by a local carpenter.

The wall on the right had a relief world map, made by Olga, using the raising compound she used for her Chinese lacquer process. It was then painted gold and an antiquing glaze applied to resemble gold leather wall paper.

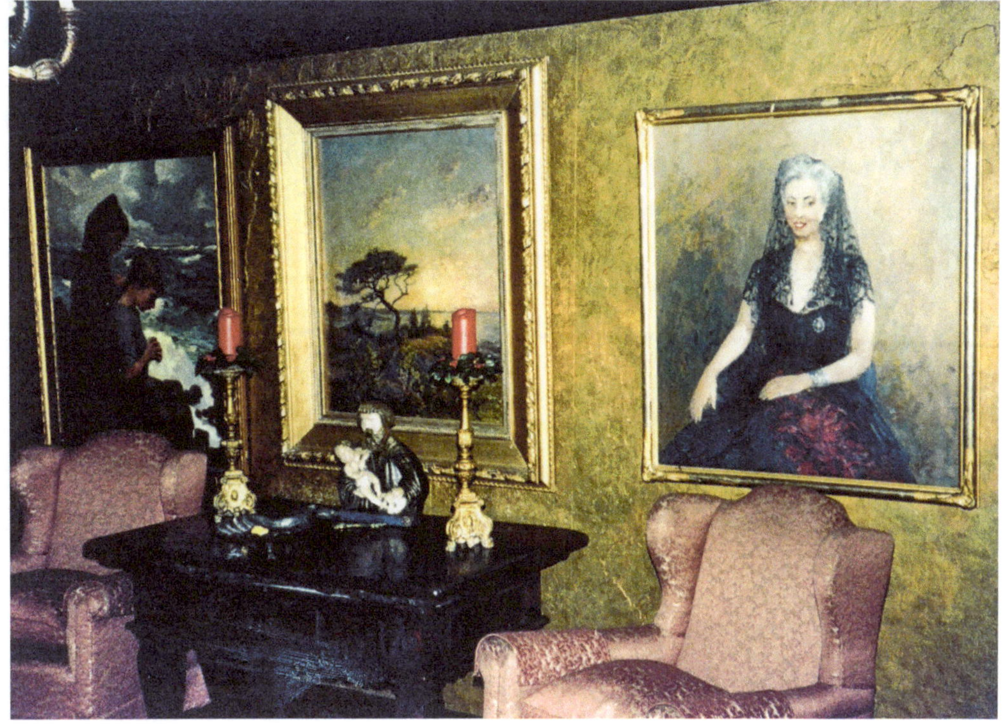

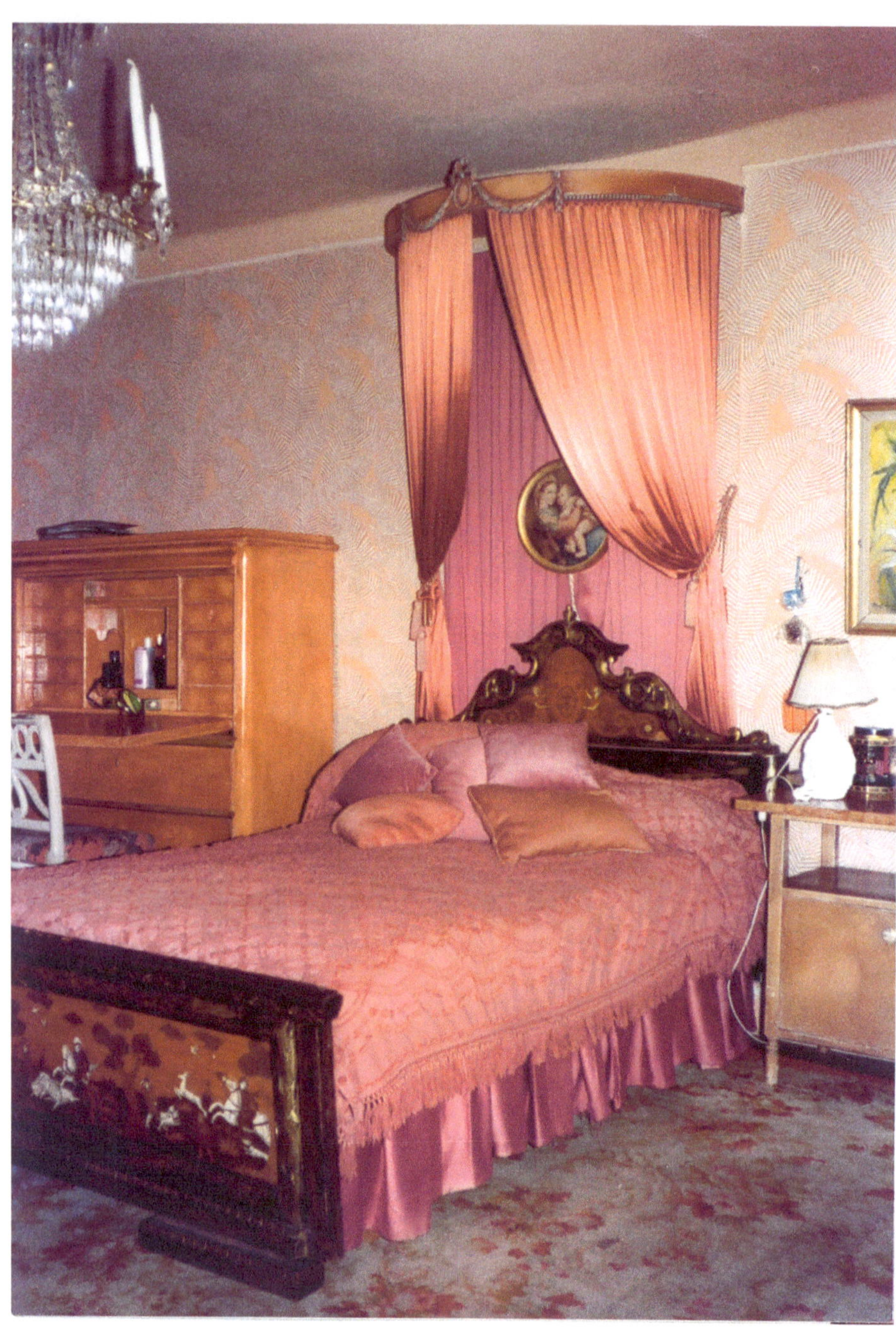

THE MASTER BEDROOM

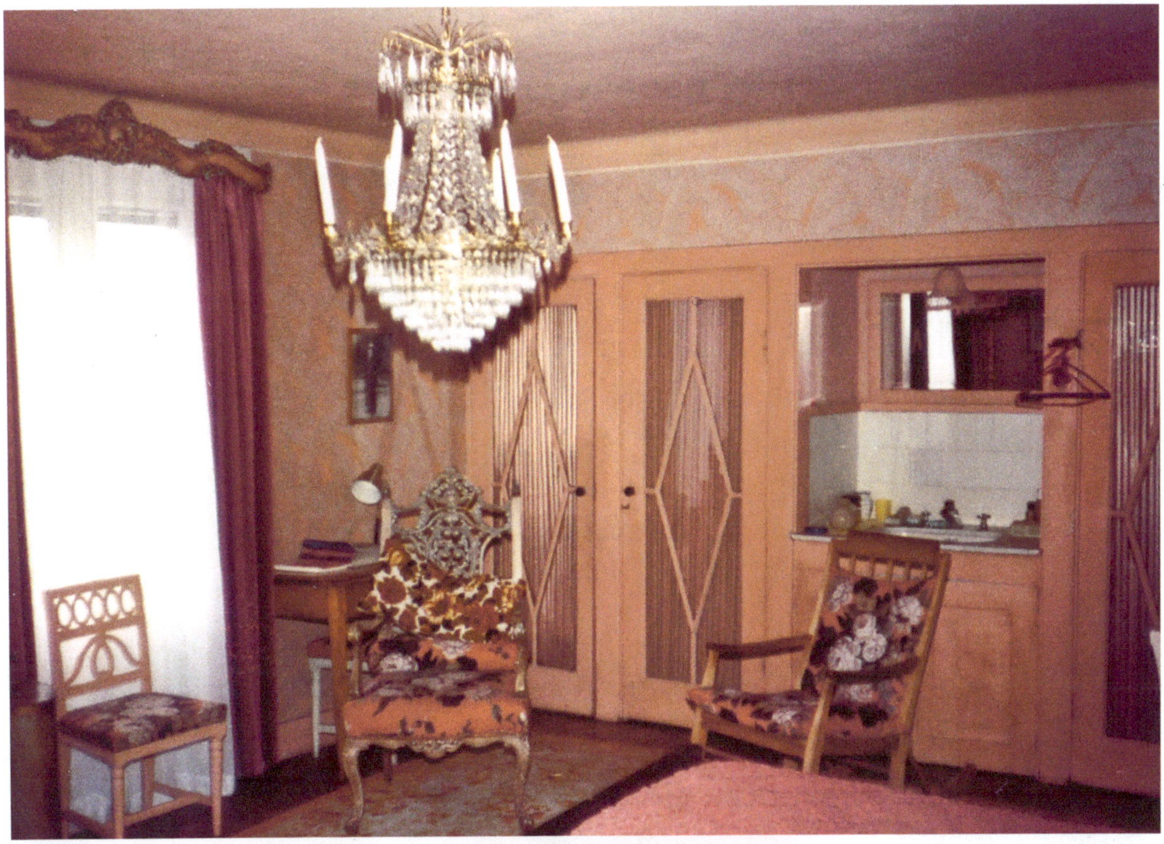

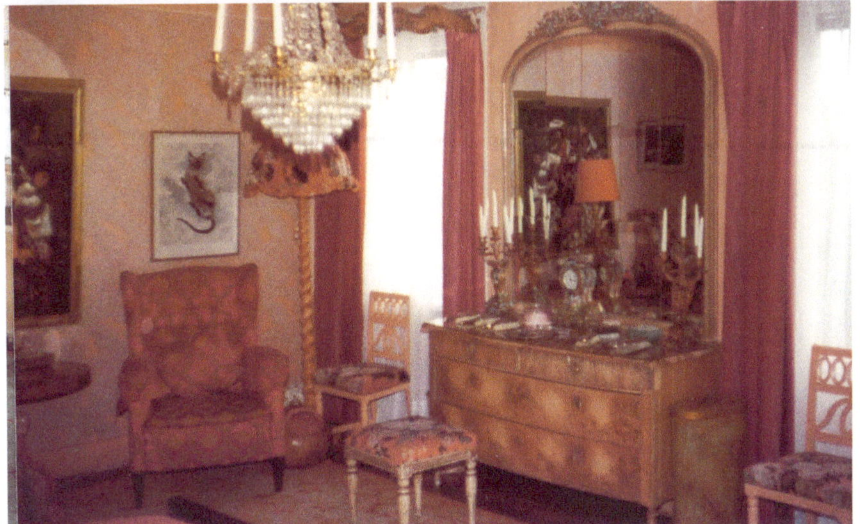

Olga later in life.

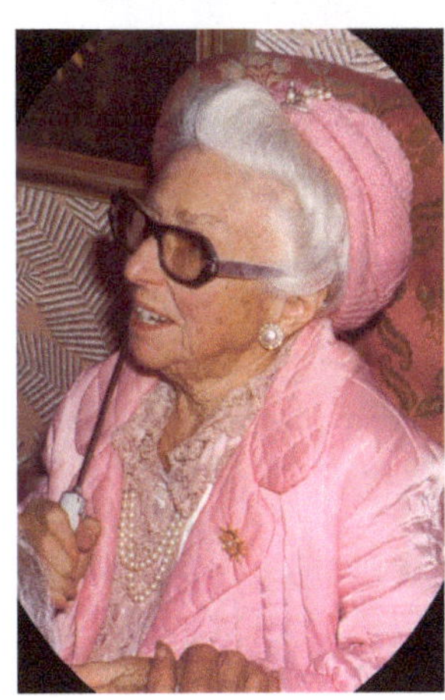

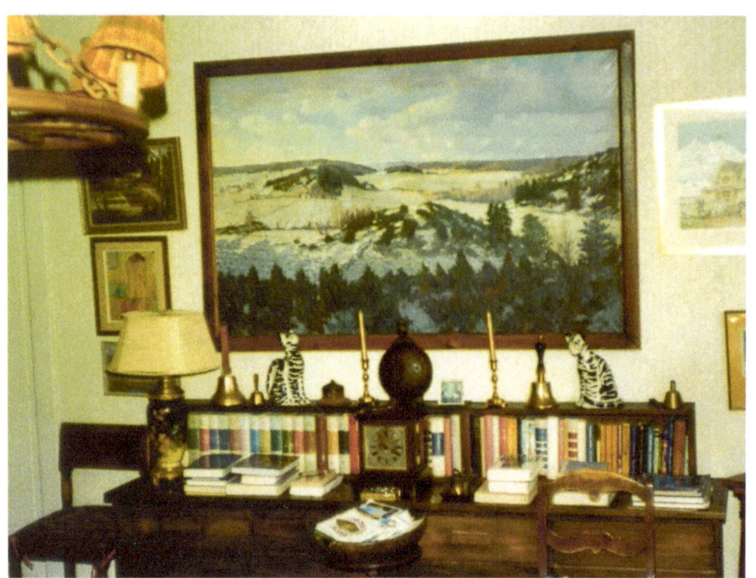

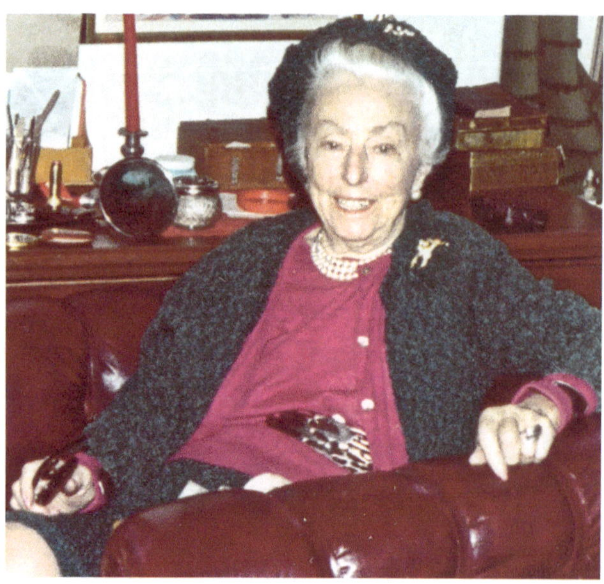

THE MÅÅTORP ROOM

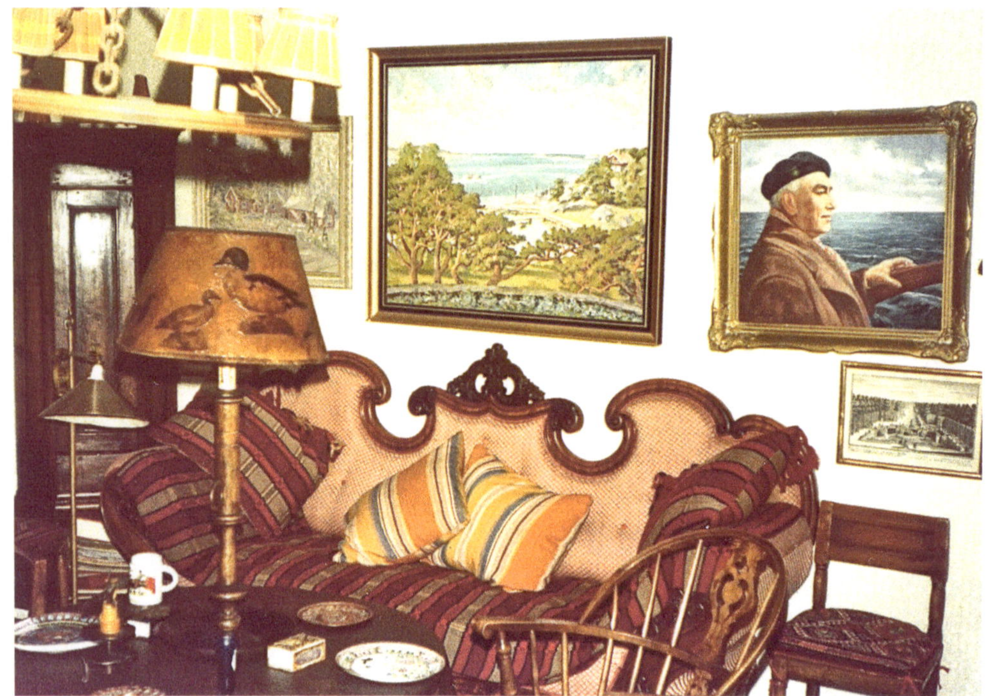

After Folke died and his hunting lodge "Måå-torp" was sold, one of the bedrooms at Lysholmen was converted into an upstairs sitting room furnished with the rustic furniture from Mååtorp.

For Olga, this was a much loved room, it reminded her of Folke. Also it was convenient, as she got older, to have a sitting room near her bedroom.

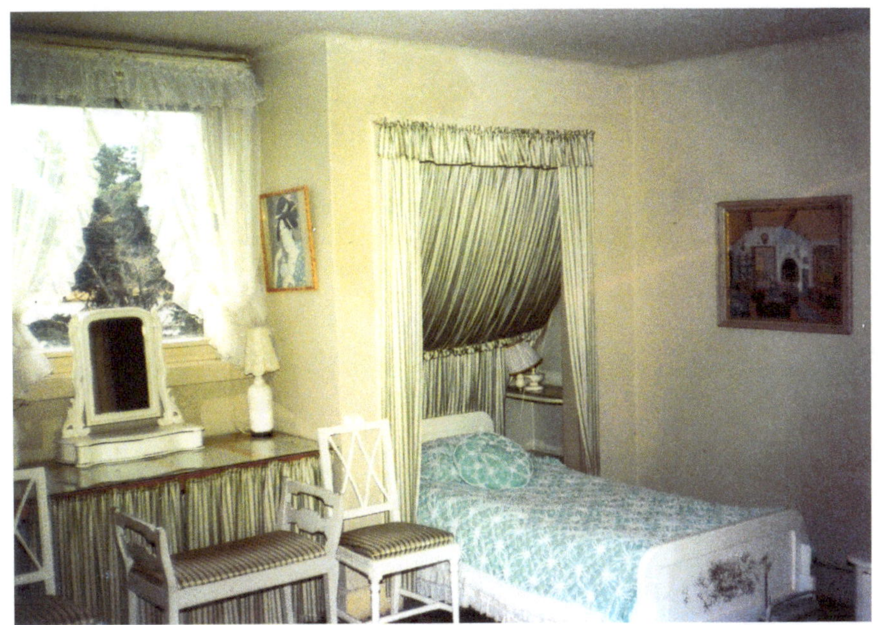

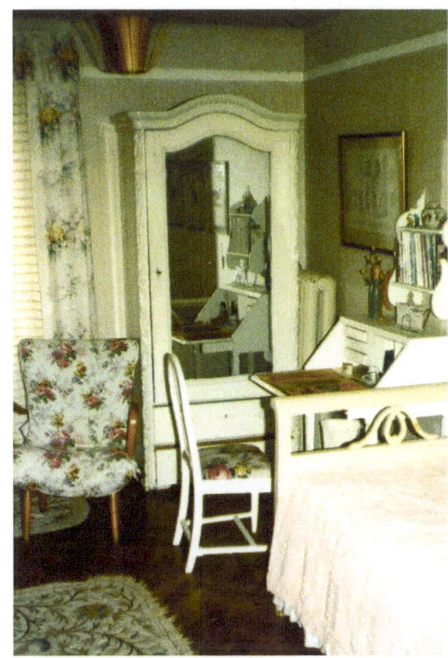

BEDROOMS

Above:
This bedroom was called "The Sibylla Room" after the Swedish Princess Sibylla who stayed here.

Above right:
Another bedroom on the second floor.

Right:
One of the three bedrooms on the third floor.

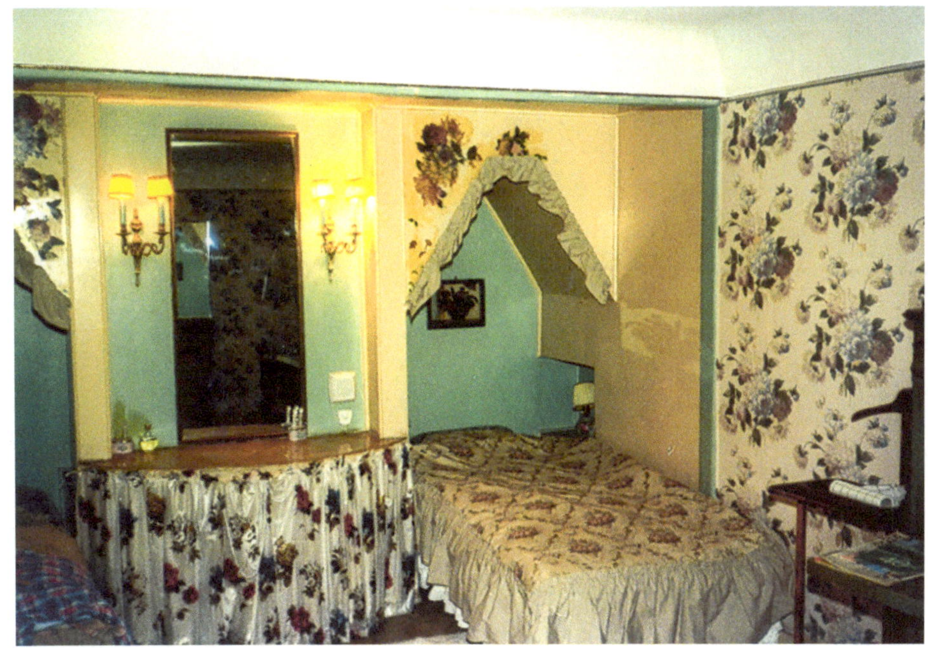

THE CELLAR

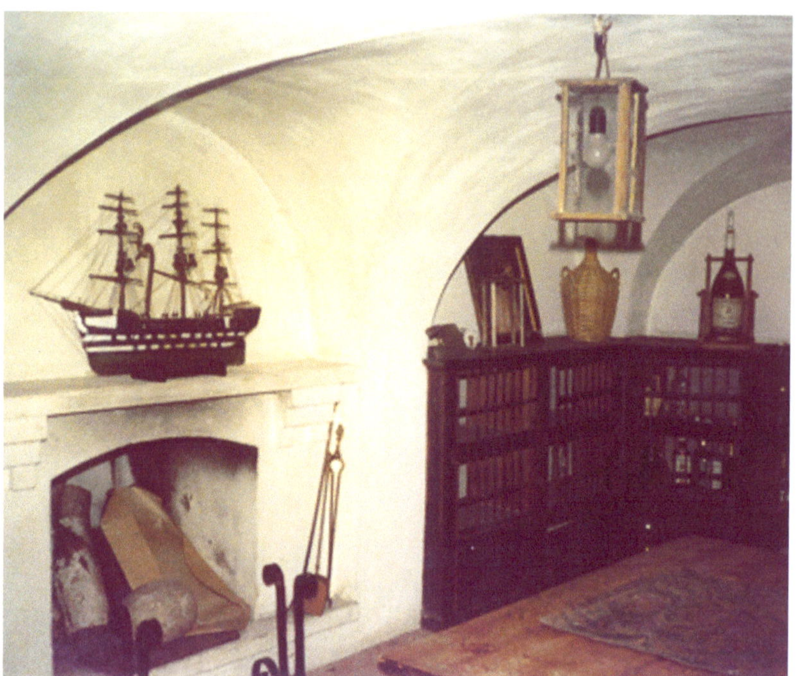

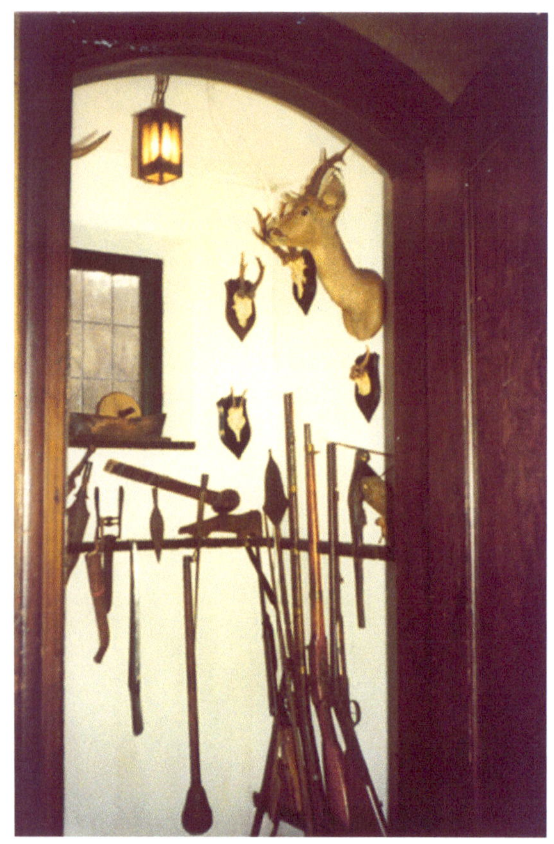

The rustic cellar was a favourite place for cray-fish parties. The billiard table was also housed here in another room until Folke later moved it to his hunting lodge Mååtorp.

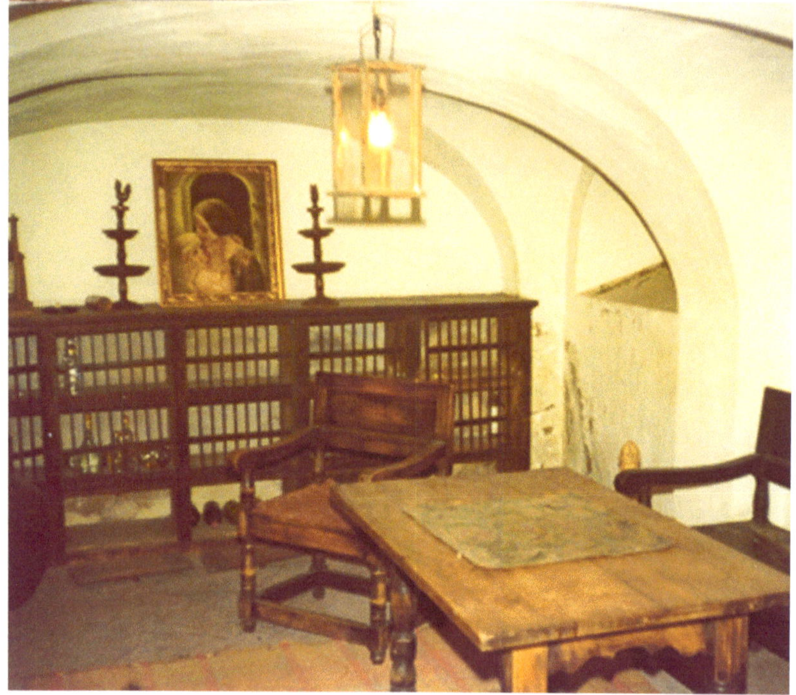

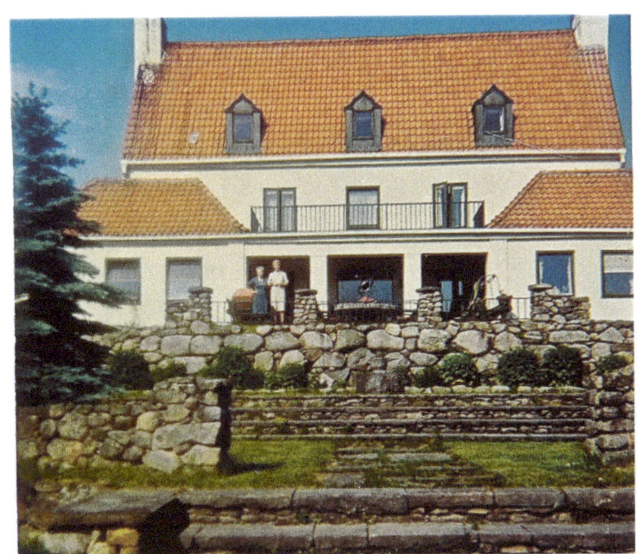

THE LOGGIA

The Loggia was a perfect place for a warm summer days with a cooling breeze coming in from the sea.

Below:
Olga with friend, Marian Lyons Smith, mother of the novelist, Donovan O'Malley.

Note the wrought iron table in the back, one of the many uses Olga made of the garden fences from Avenyn in Gothenburg that she bought from a scrap yard for a pittance.

Left: Olga and her old friend Ingrid Keiller stand in front of the loggia, looking out over the sea.

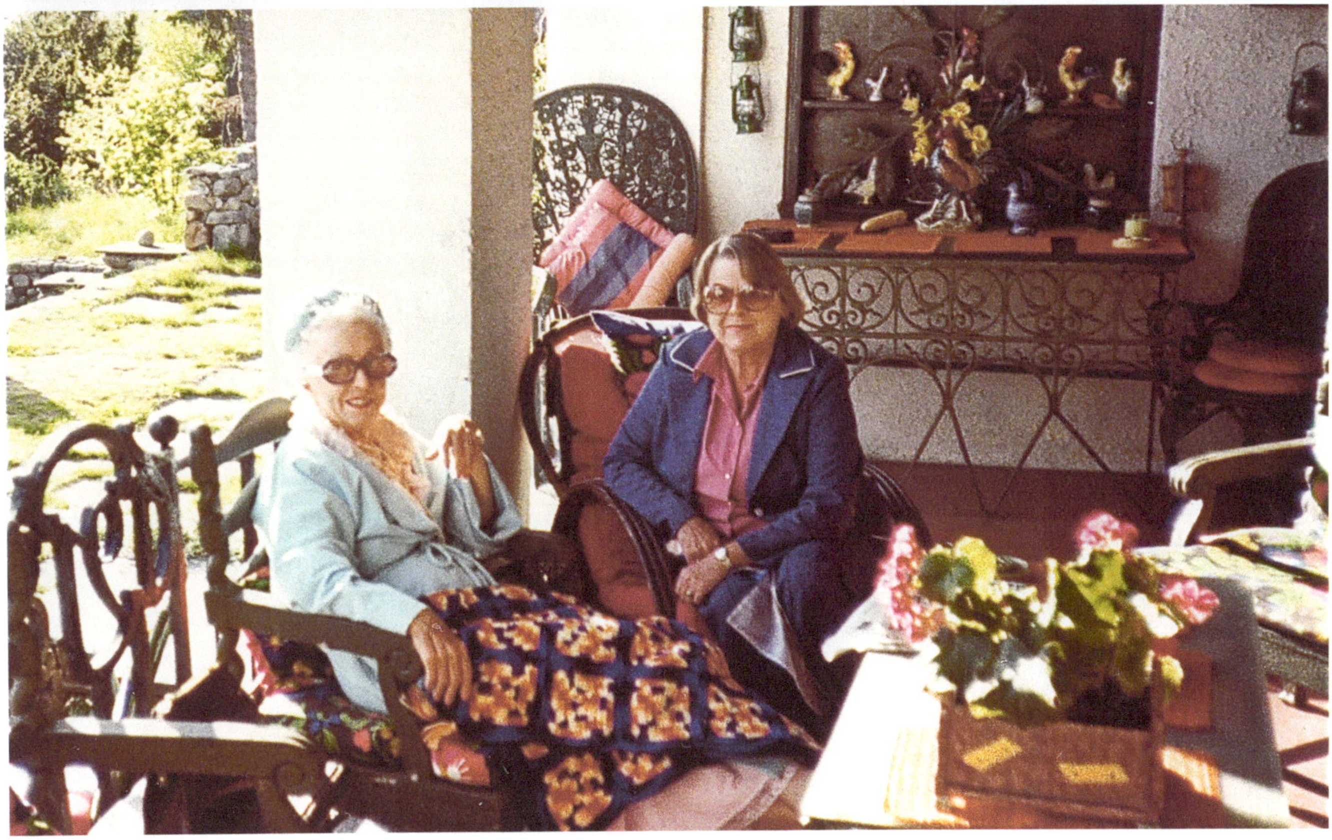

THE KITCHEN AND SERVING HALL

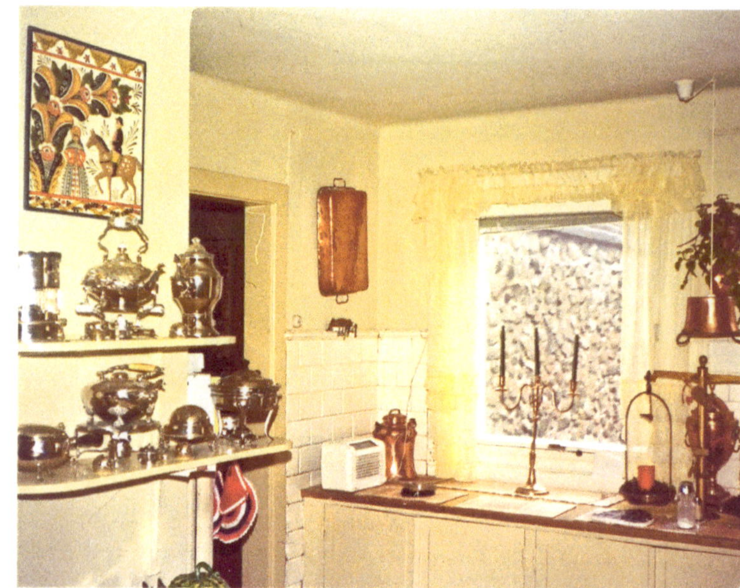

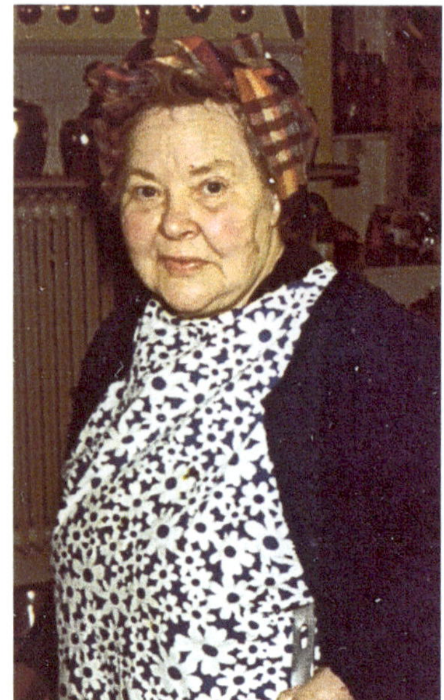

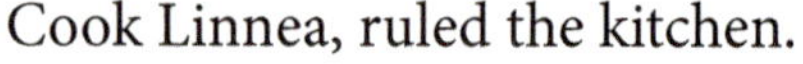

Cook Linnea, ruled the kitchen.

Olga (right) always sat in that particular place when she had breakfast in the serving hall, a room between the kitchen and the dining room.

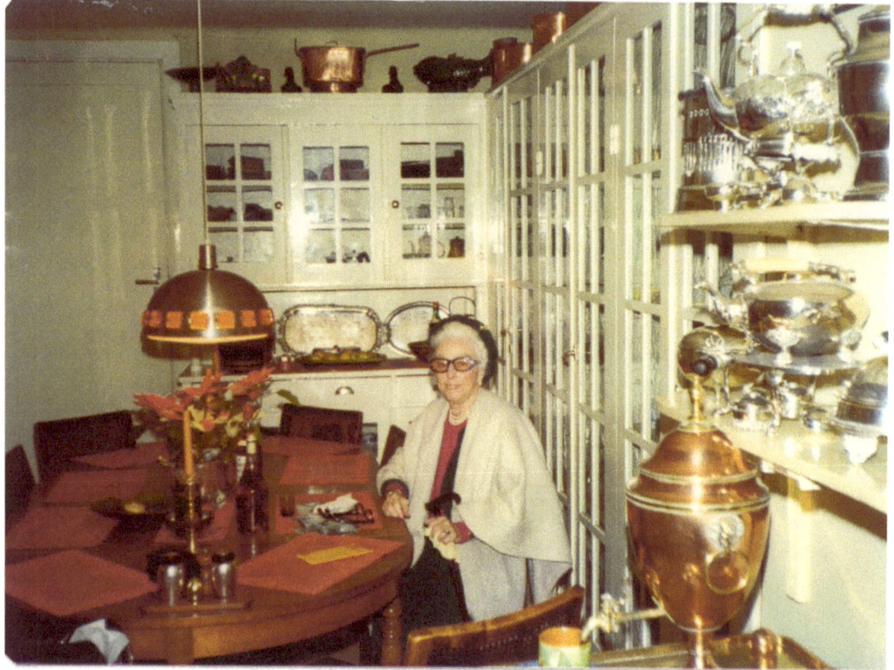

GROWING THINGS

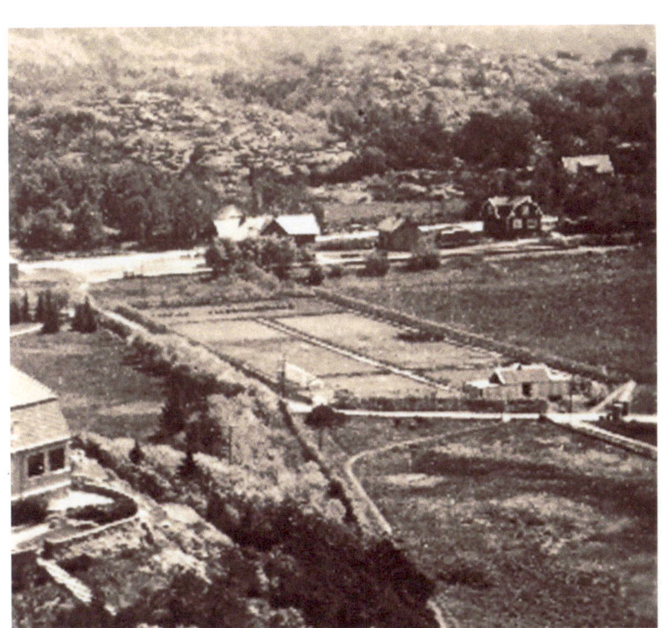

Below Lysholmen, a level field close to the main road was used for a large vegetable garden. The area had been sectioned with wide stone paths and fertile soil brought in, creating a very large area to grow vegetables.

A chicken house was also built. During World War 2 when food was rationed, eggs were sent from Lysholmen to studying daughter Gunilla (my mother), at Uppsala. The eggs saved her, she wrote to her mother, Olga.

The green house produced thousands of peaches, grapes and tomatoes. Below, Olga and daughter, Gunilla, are cleaning homegrown vegetables on the Lysholmen loggia ca 1940.

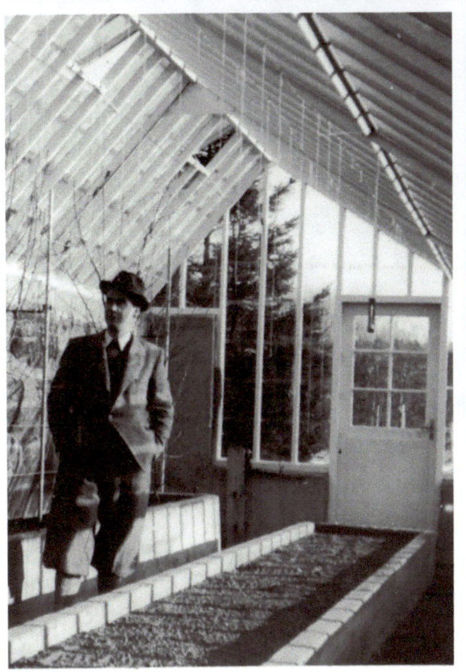

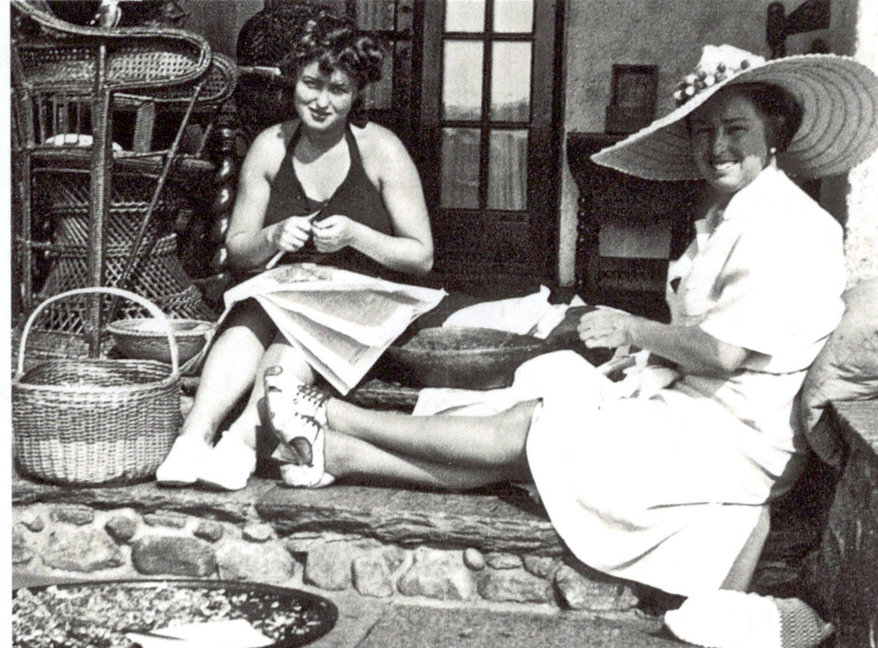

LYSHOLMEN
A CHILDREN'S PARADISE

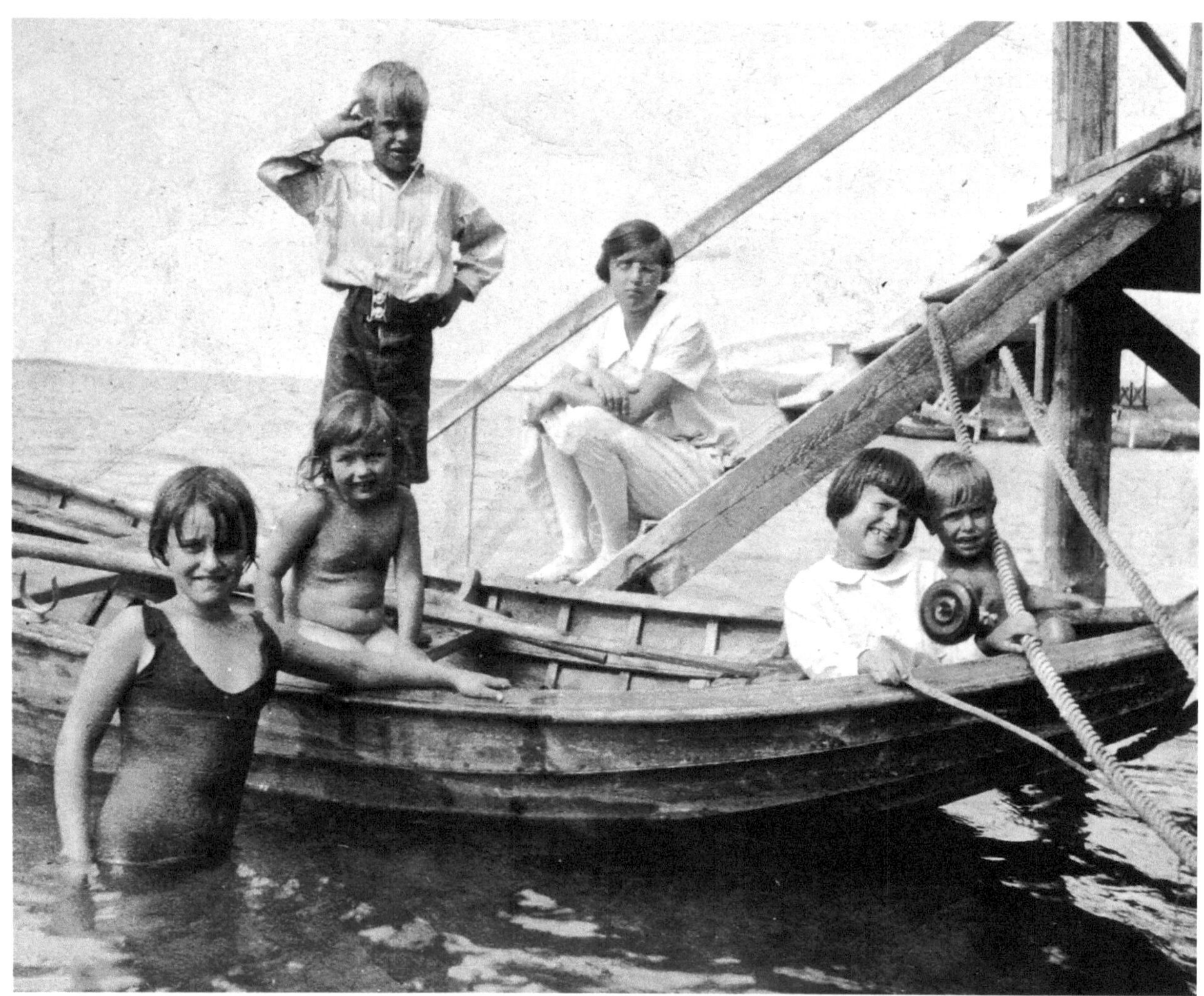

Olga and Folke's children from left: Sonja, Gunilla, Bo-Erling, Mary, Sigrid and Claes-Herbert.

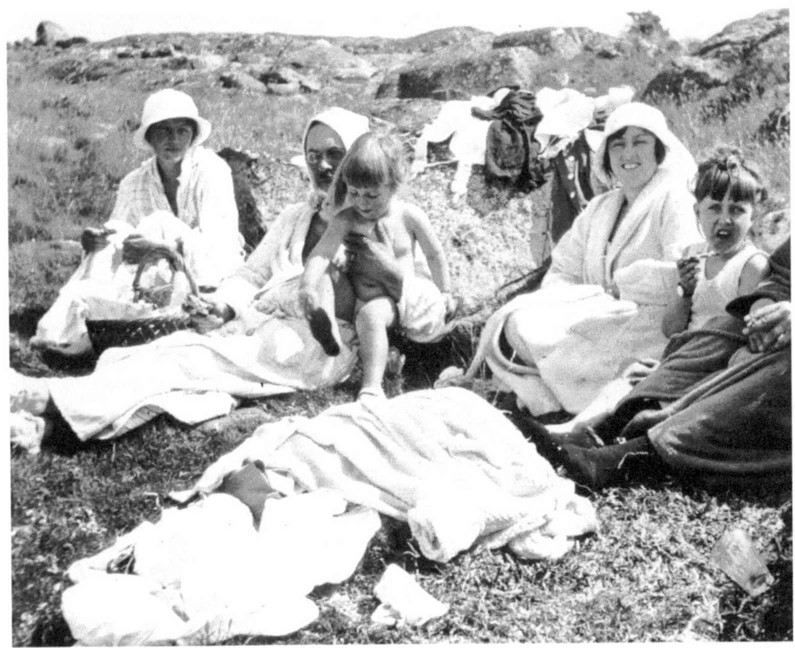

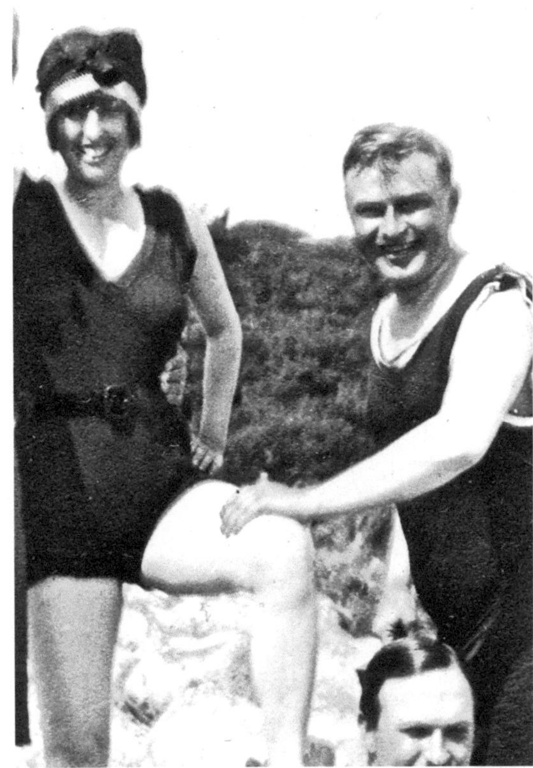

ARCHIPELAGO EXCURSIONS

Olga and Folke with friends, enjoying an excursion in the Särö archipelago ca 1925

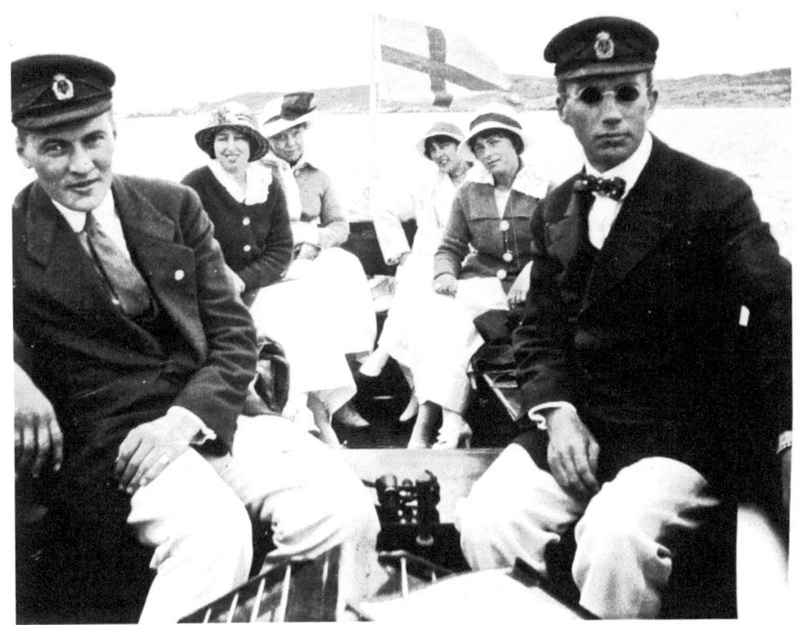

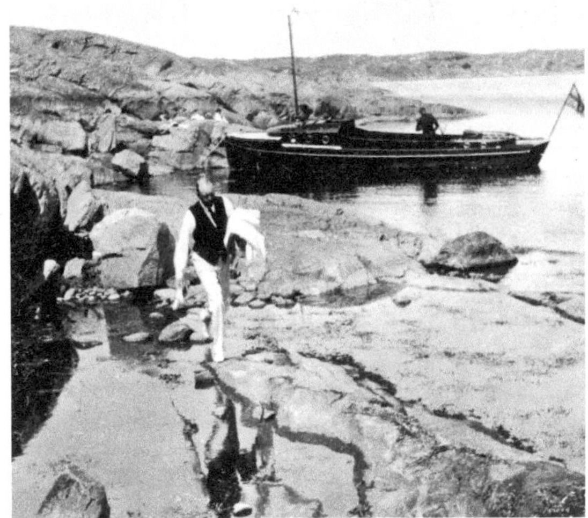

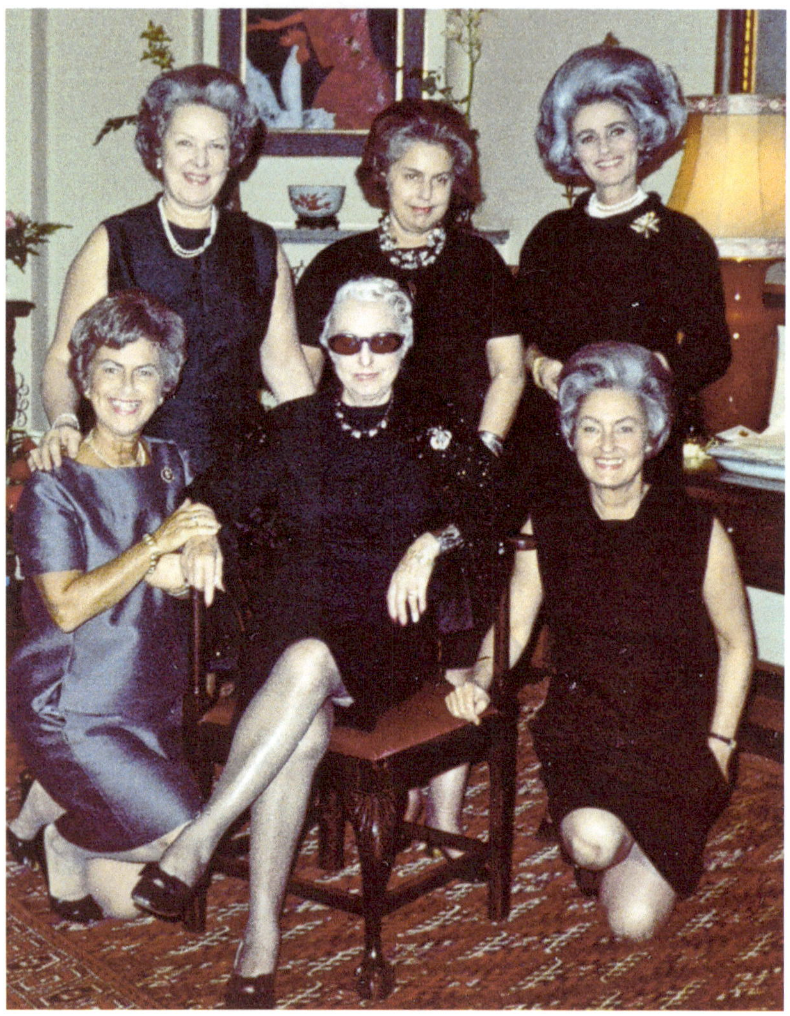

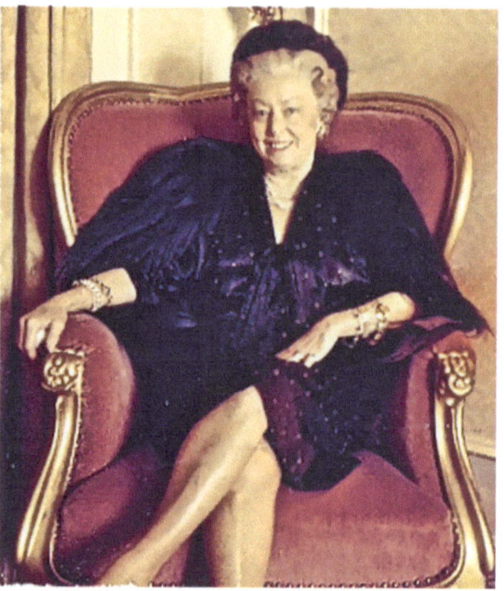

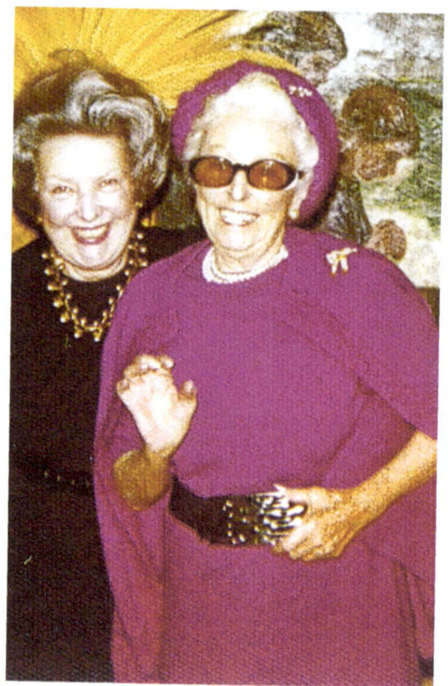

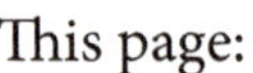

This page:
Top left: Olga and her daughters in 1970. From left: Sigrid, Anita, Mary, Sonja, Gunilla, mother of editor, Leif Södergren.
Top right: Olga in her black monkey fur cape
Right: Olga and oldest daughter Anita.

OLGA

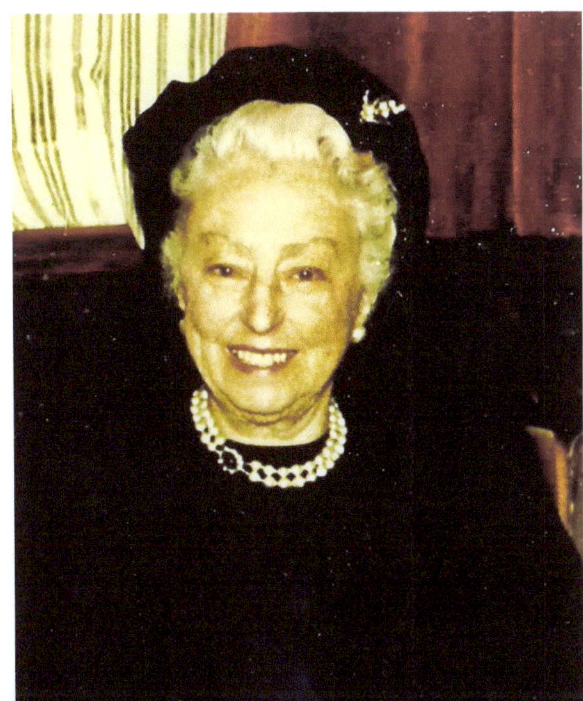

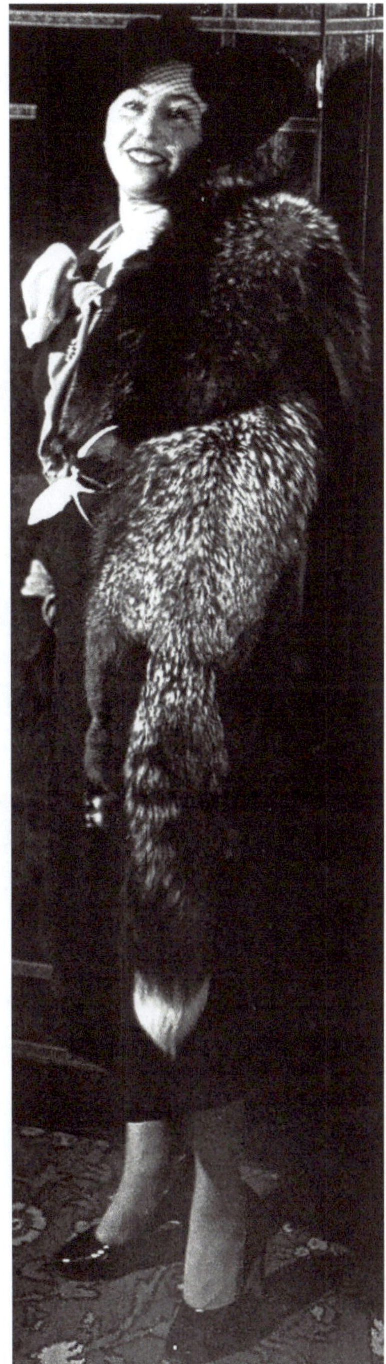

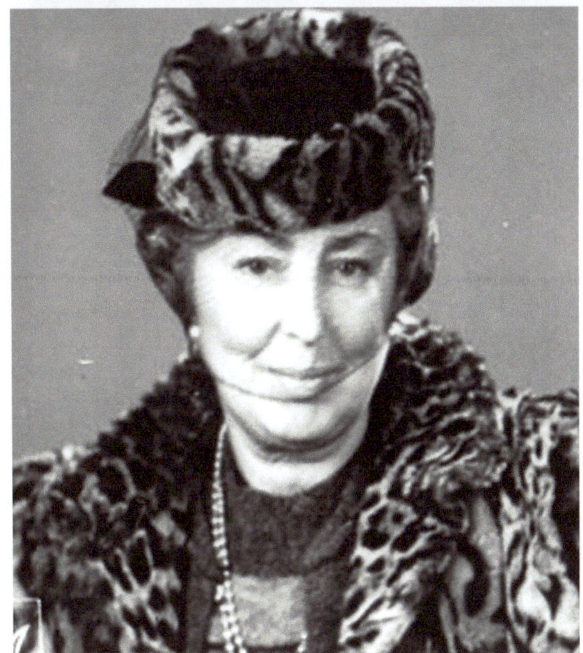

OLGA, MOTHER OF NINE

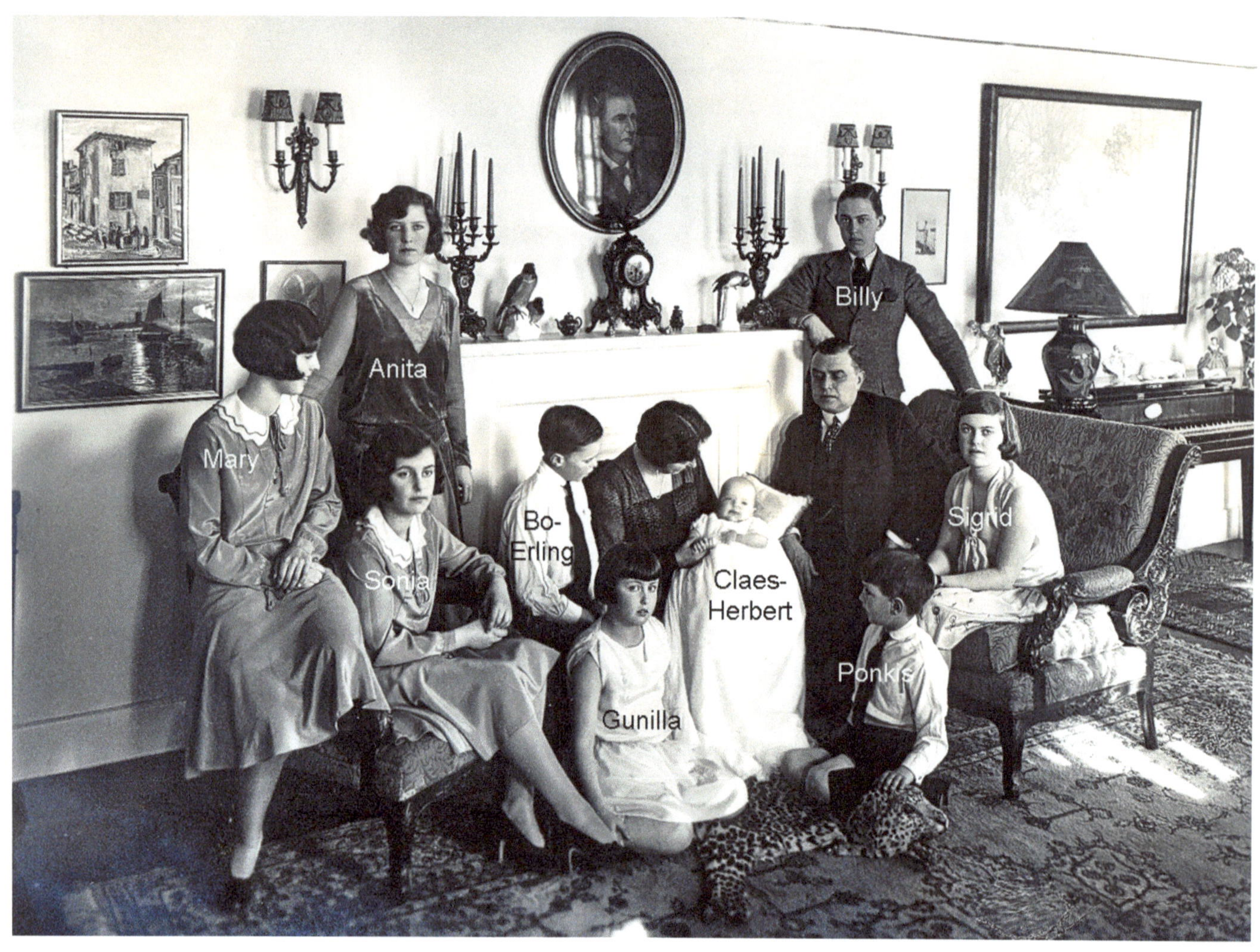

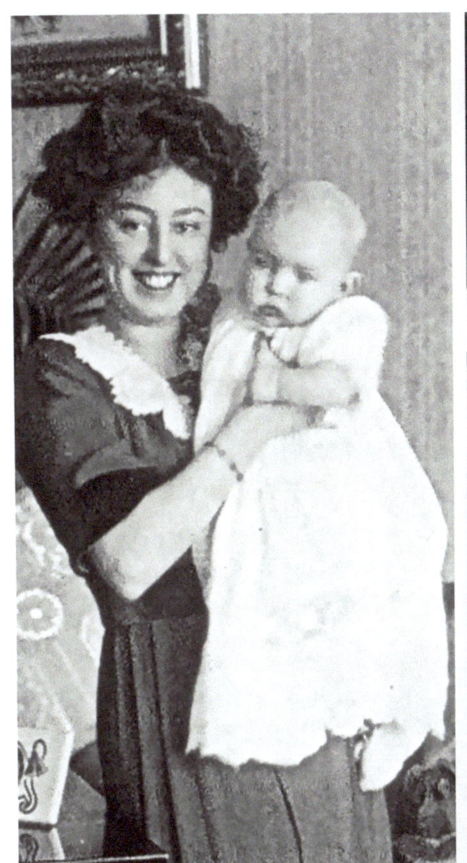

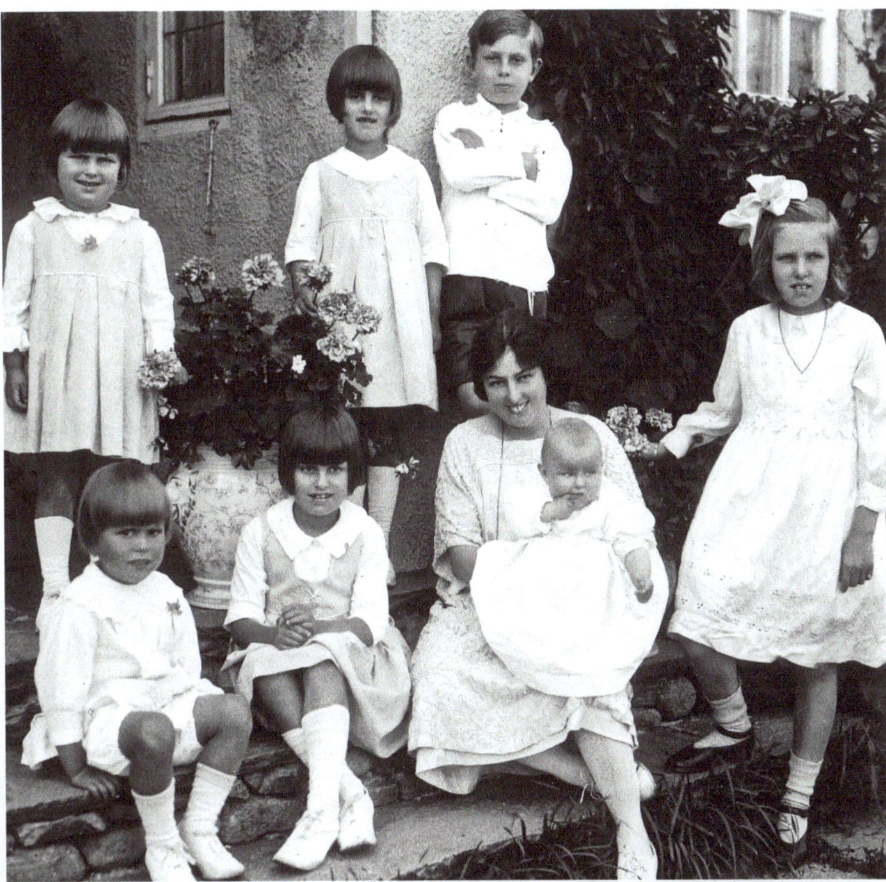

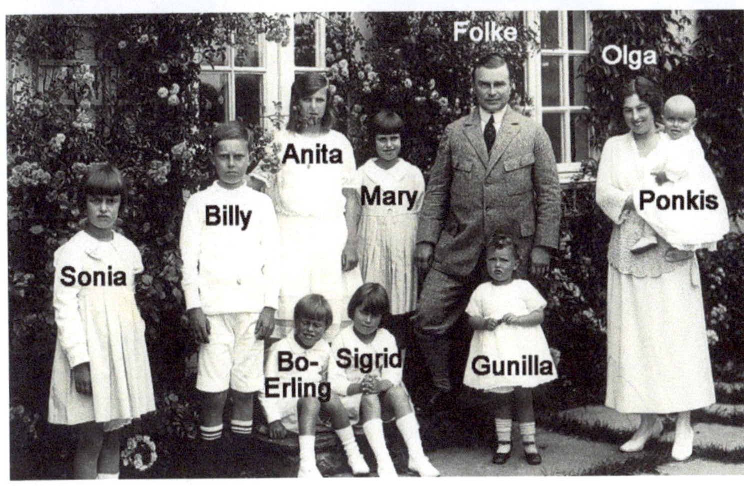
Folke
Olga
Anita
Billy
Mary
Ponkis
Sonia
Bo-
Erling
Sigrid
Gunilla

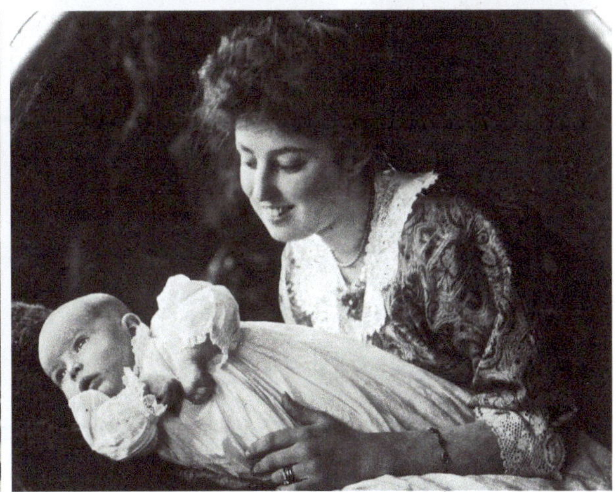

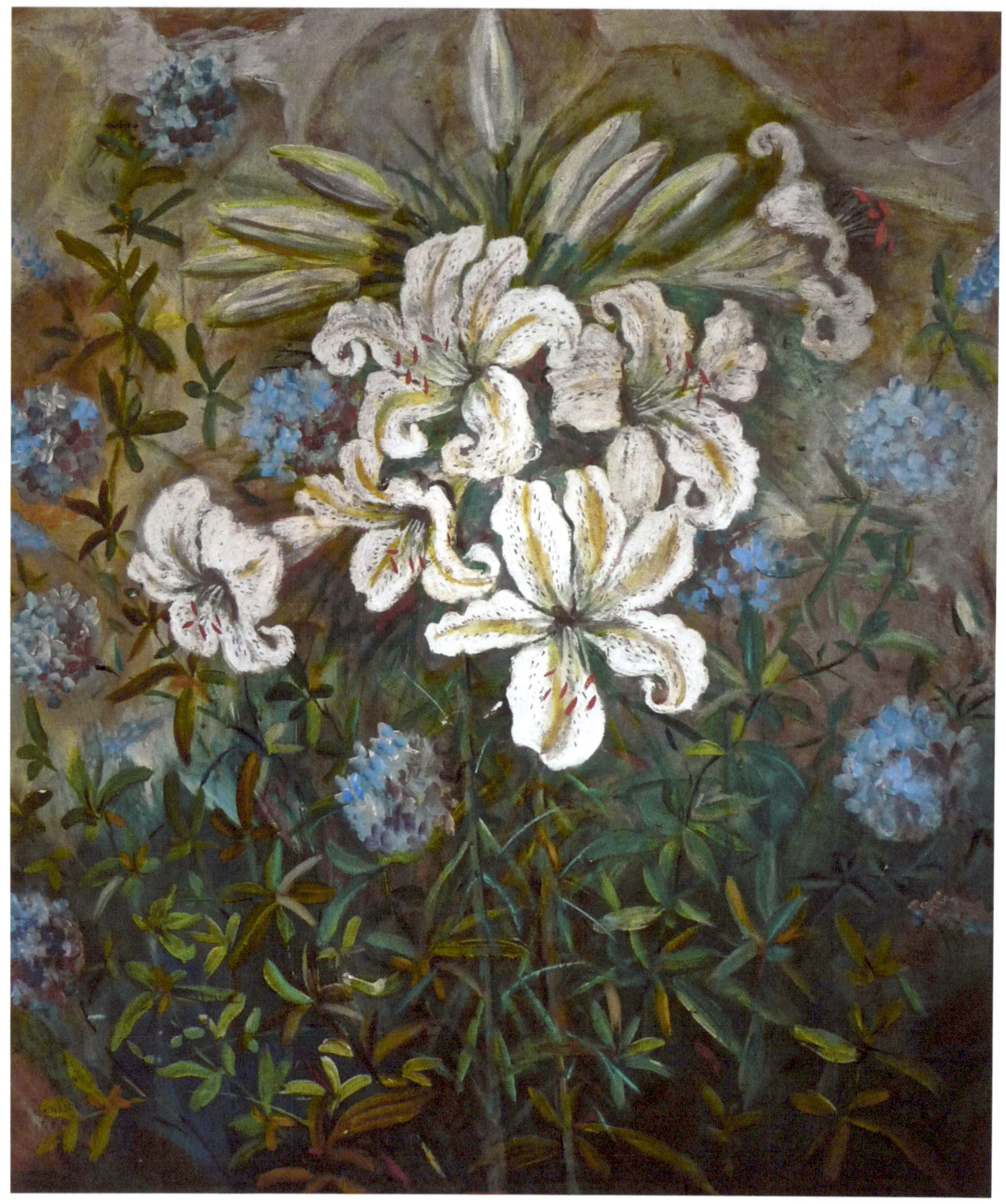

OLGA, AS ARTIST

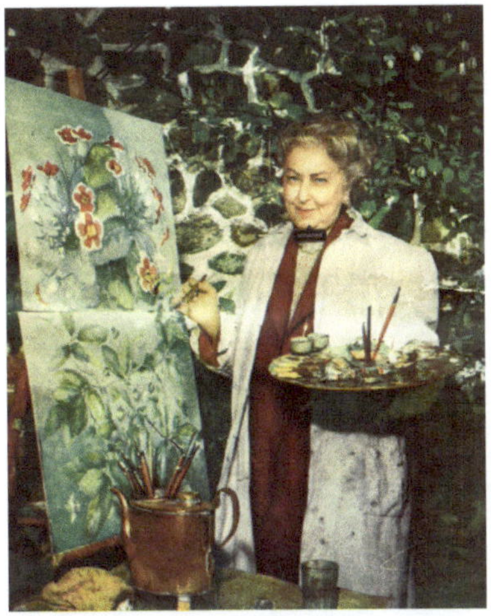

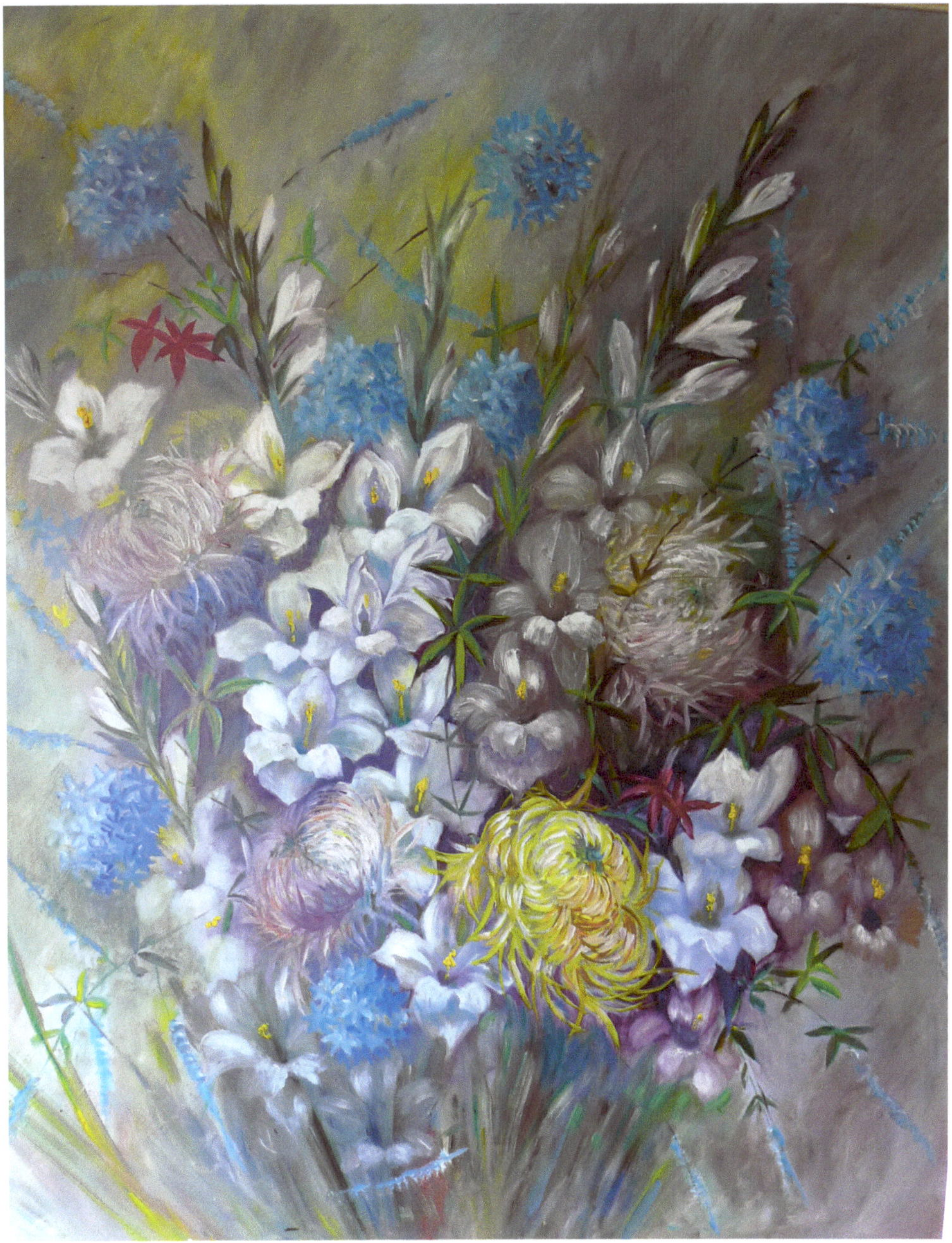

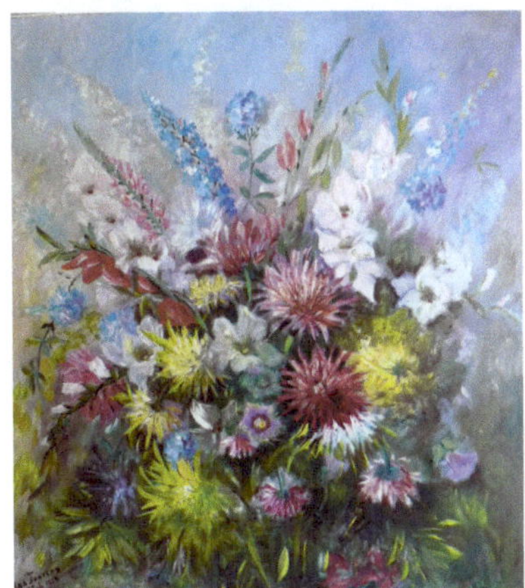

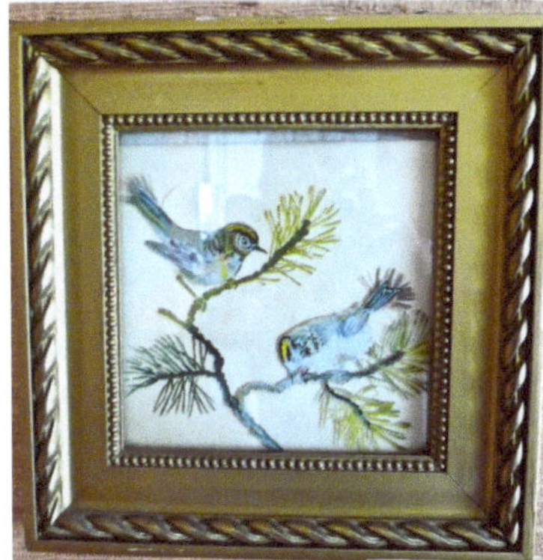

OLGA'S CHINESE LACQUER

In London, Olga took lessons in Chinese Lacquer work and she became so proficient that antique shops in Gothenburg took her work for the real thing. One must have excellent eyesight and a sure hand for this extremely detailed work.

The Swedish King Gustav V liked Olga's bridge tables so much (bottom right) that he was given two. Olga's daughters also learned this skill.

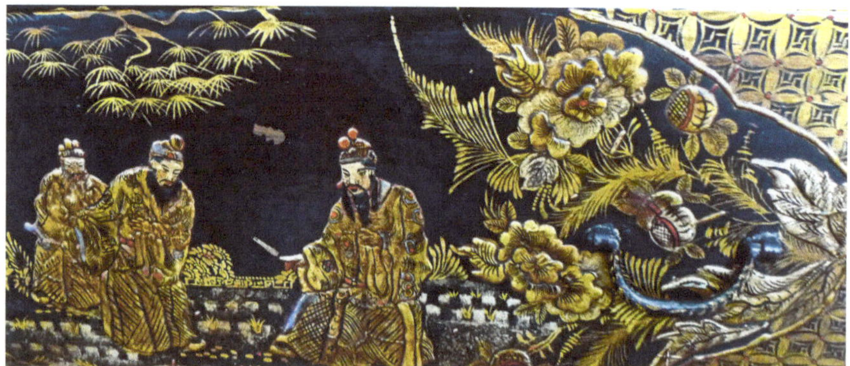

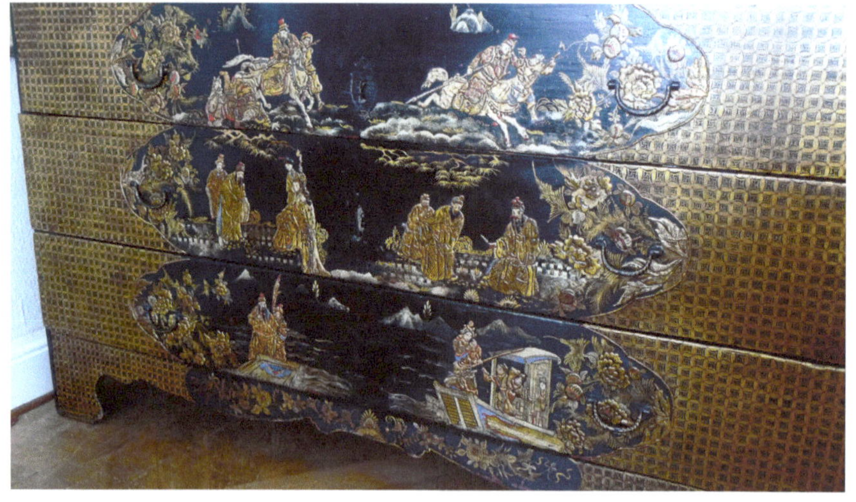

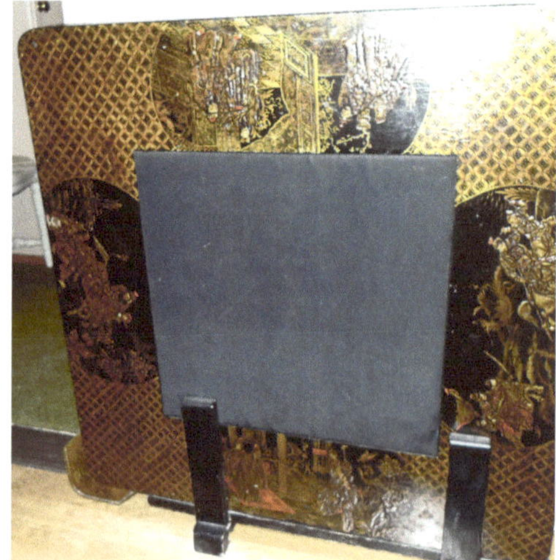

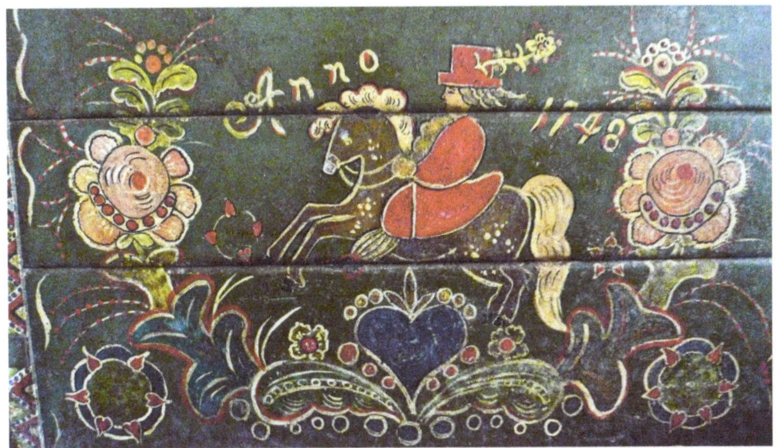

OLGA'S SWEDISH FOLK ART

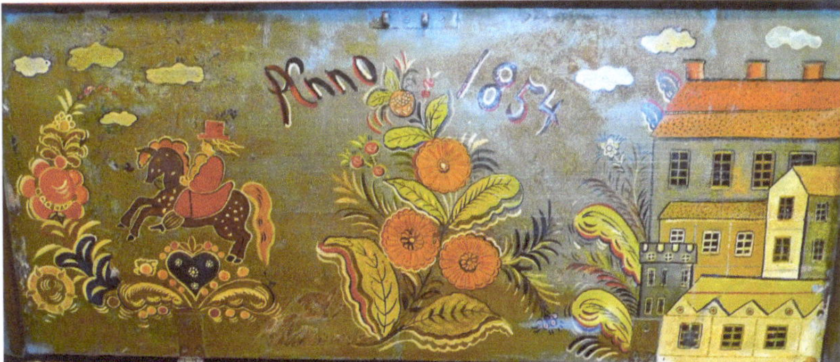

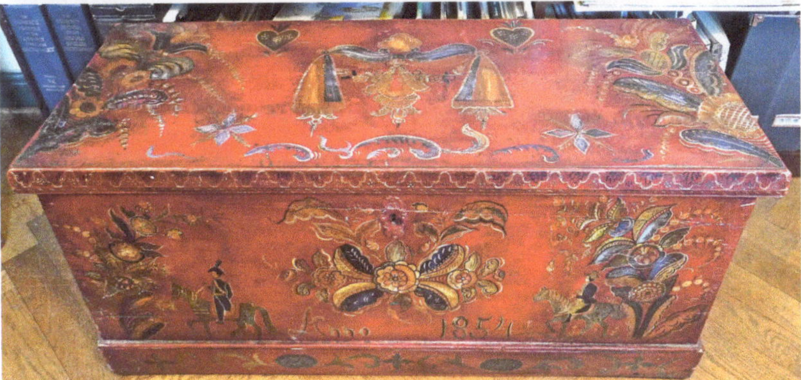

The red chest was one of many gifts from Olga to the RED CROSS over the years. My mother, Gunilla, was lucky to win it at their bazaar at Särö in 1959 (!)

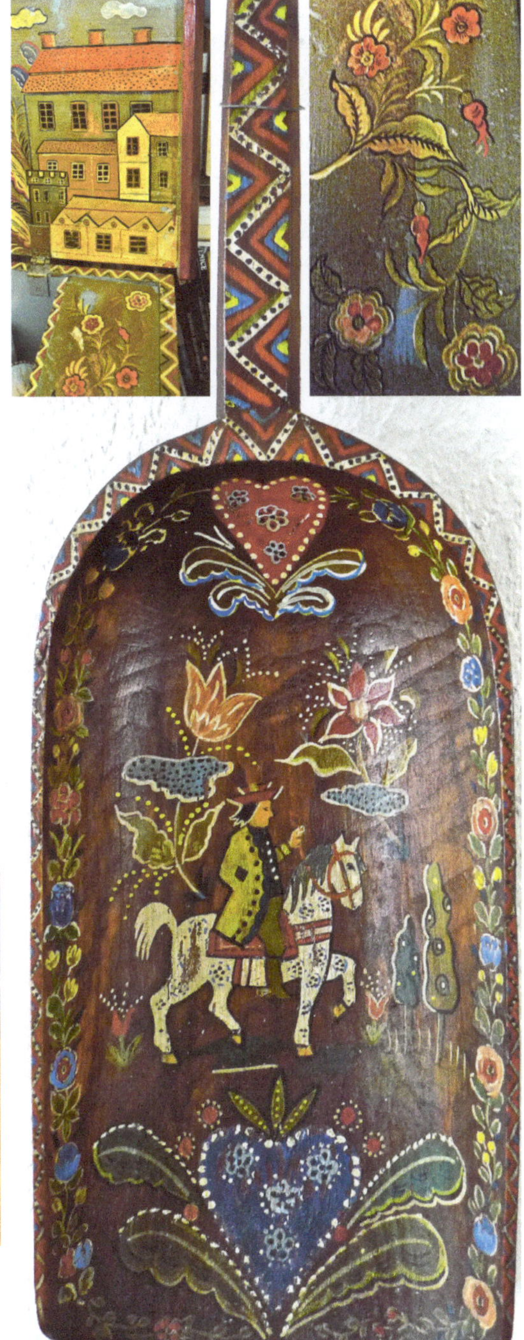

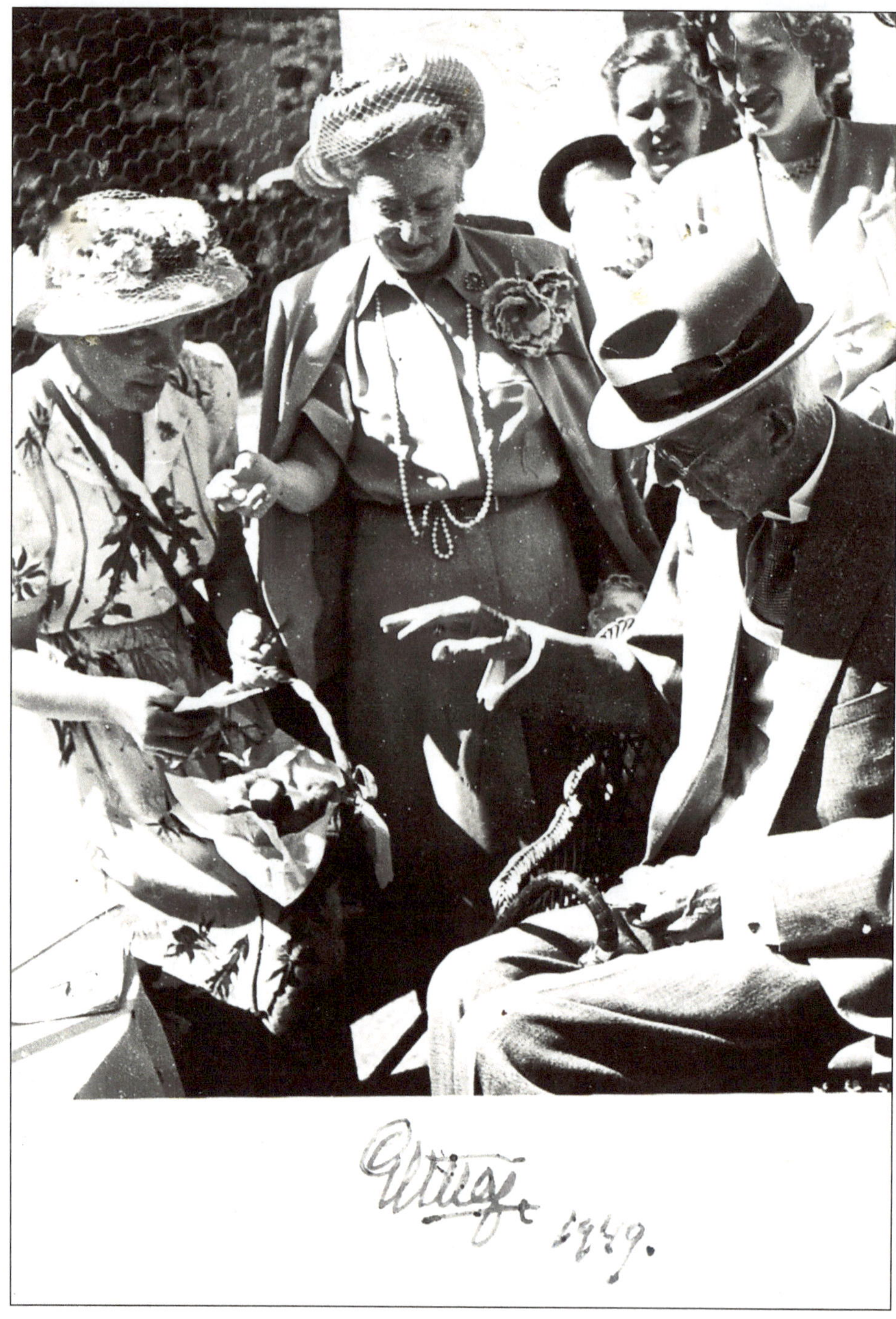

OLGA AND THE RED CROSS

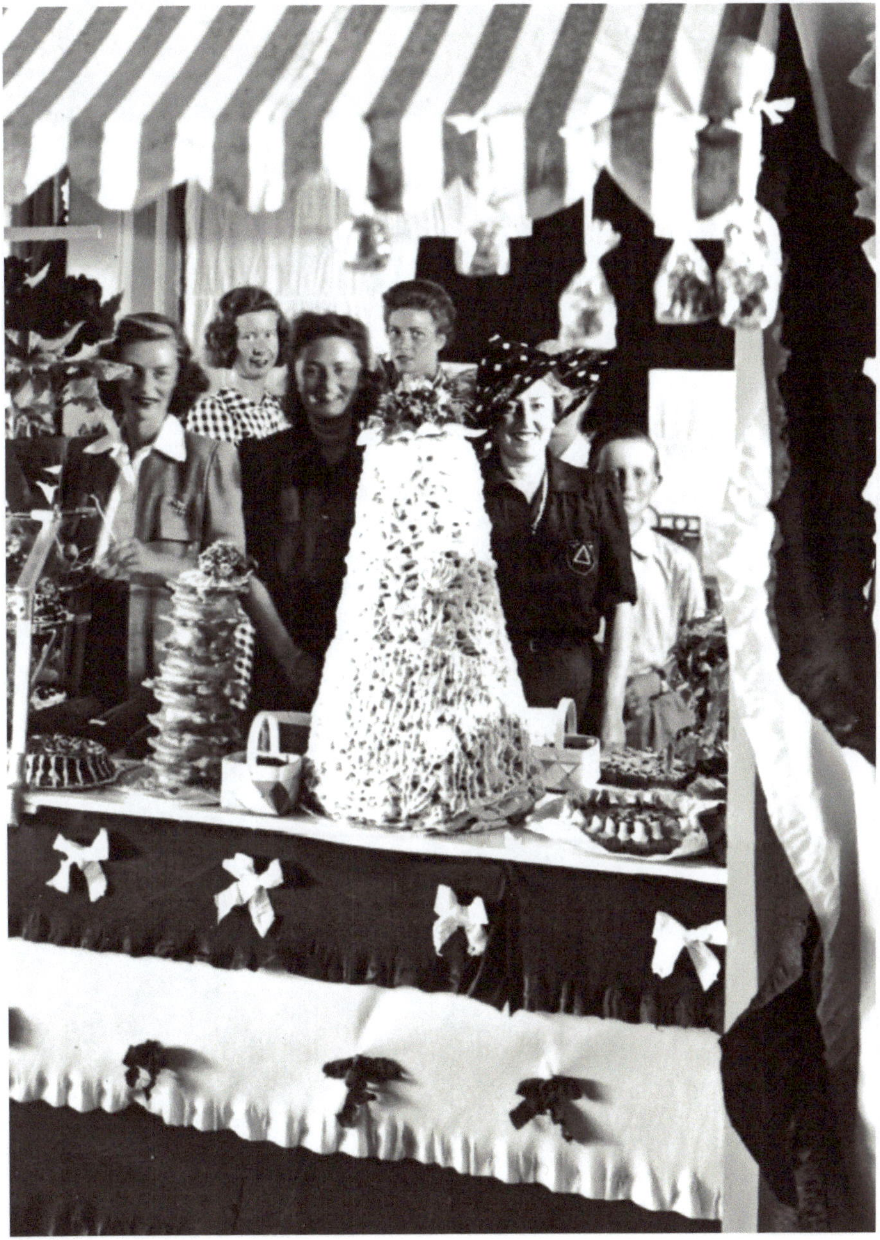

As the head of the SÄRÖ RED CROSS chapter, Olga was busy every year arranging the annual bazaar. As the Swedish King Gustav V always paid a visit, the event got maximum publicity (opposite page).

Many women in the Red Cross were engaged all year making things for the lottery and Olga oversaw it all .

Left:
Olga (in dotted hat with daughter Gunilla beside) at the Red Cross bazaar cake stand. They stand behind the magnificent "Spette-kaka", a regional delicacy which was also the King's favourite cake.

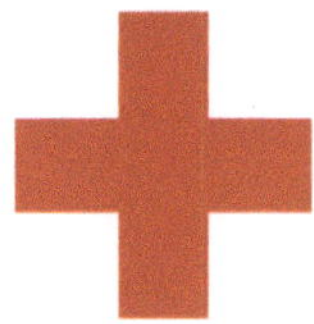

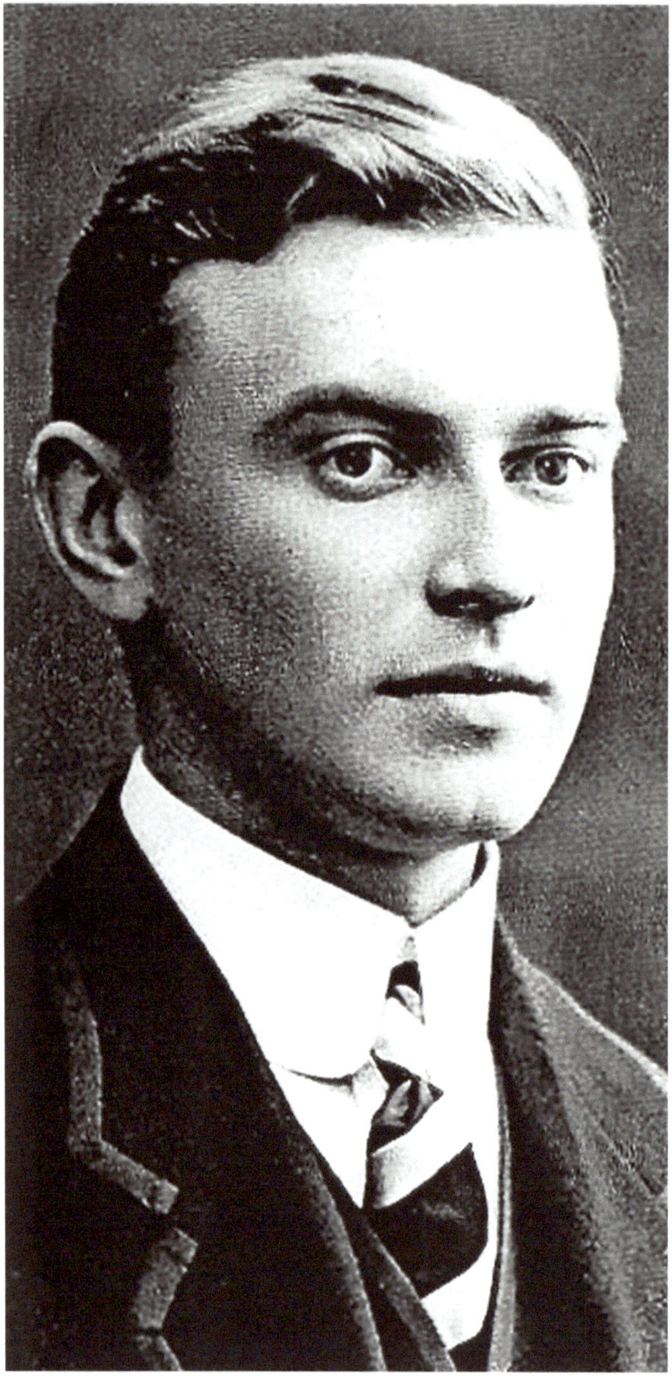

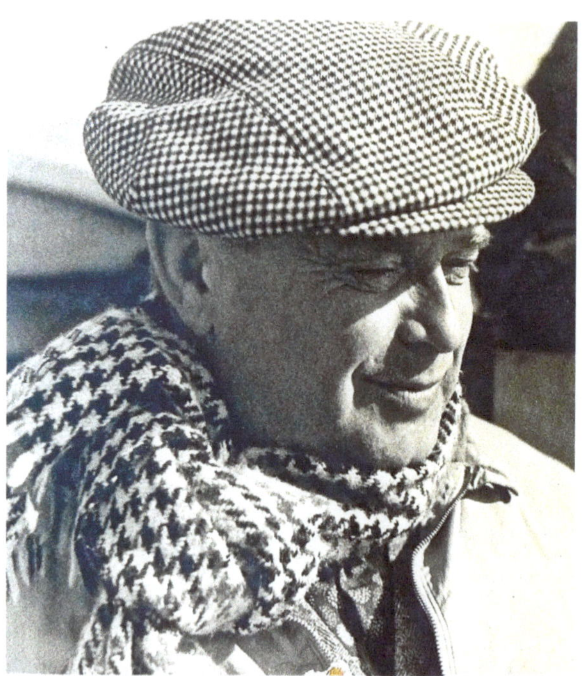

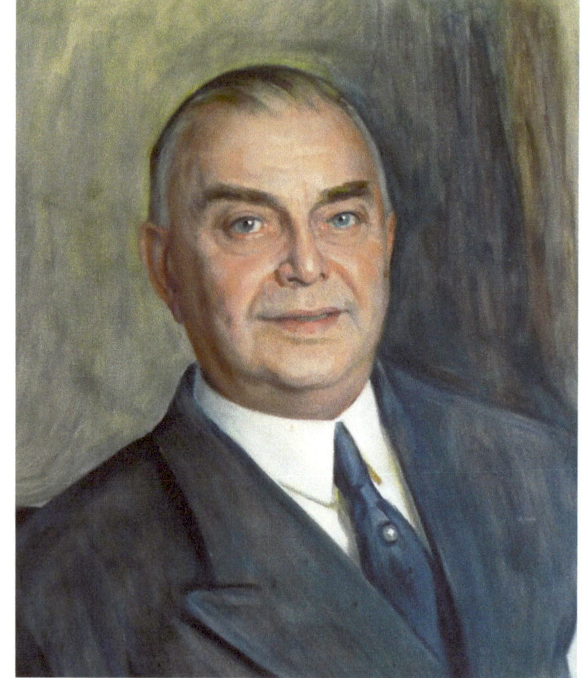

FOLKE

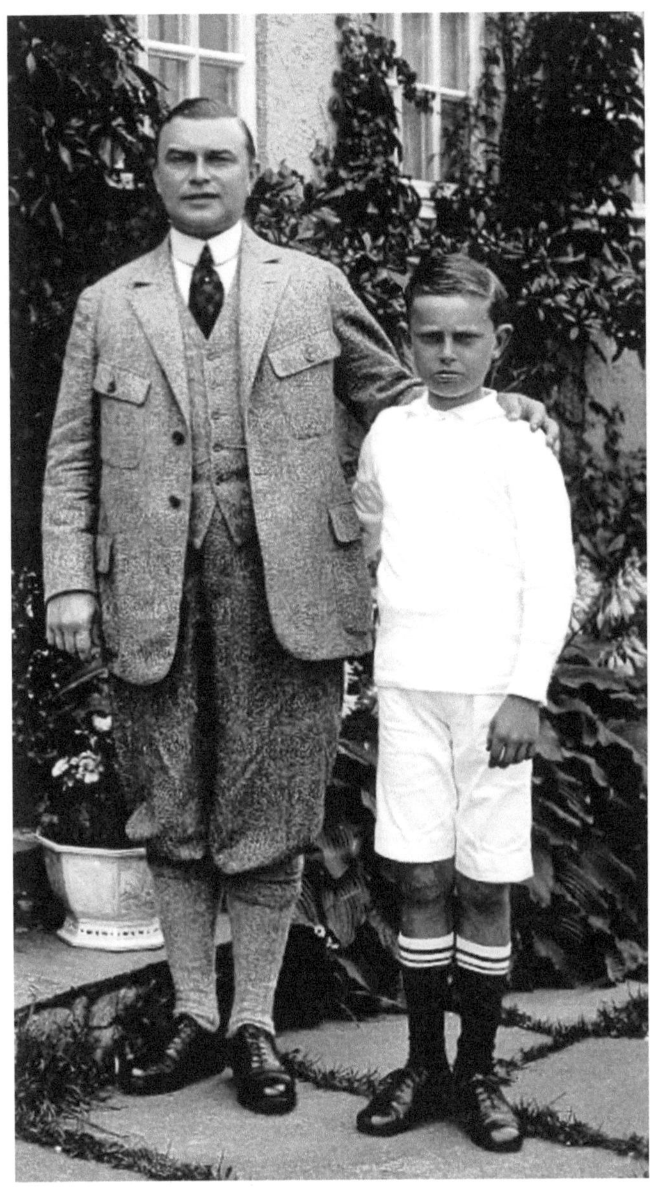

Folke with his oldest son Billy

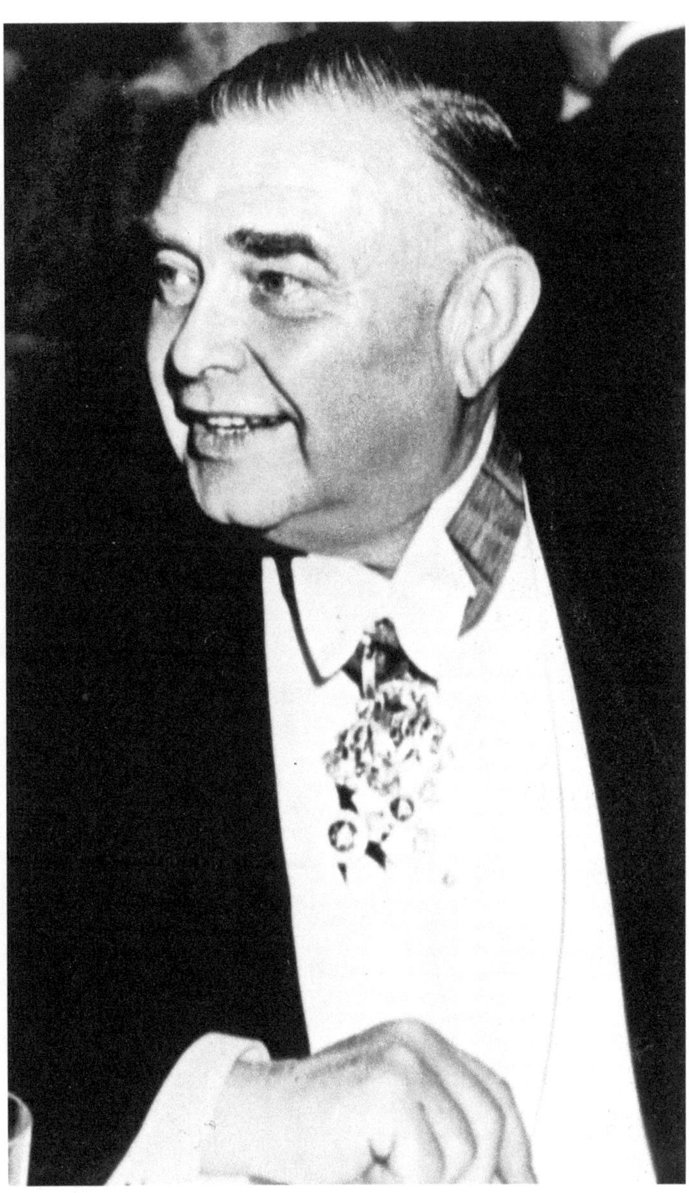

James Keiller
Dan-Axel Broström
Knut Dalman
Göran von Essen
Sven Hansson
Lars Hill-Lindquist
Henning Krafft
Lars Hedwall
Erik Lundh
Axel Nordström
Car-Eric Odelberg
Folke Ramström
Carol Wallenberg
Otto Silverschhiöld

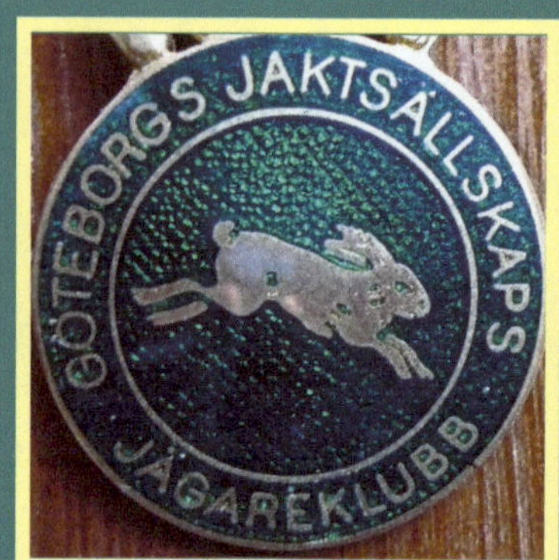

1960

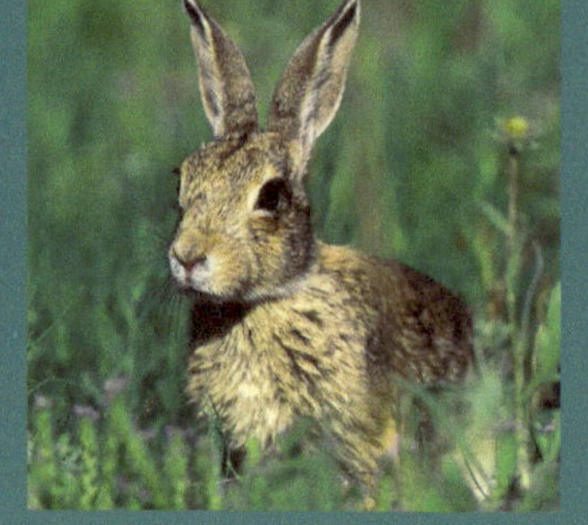

Gustaf Adolf Bratt
Gösta Dahlman
Claes Ekman
Claes Grill
Victor Hasselblad
Folke Jonsson
Georg Lithander
Fritjof Nordborg
Kurt Nordström
Sven Raab
Patrik Rydbeck
Gustaf Svensson
Erik Wijk
Per Arne Wållgren

FOLKE'S FRIENDS AND
MEMBERS OF THE HUNTING ASSOCIATION
HE BELONGED TO

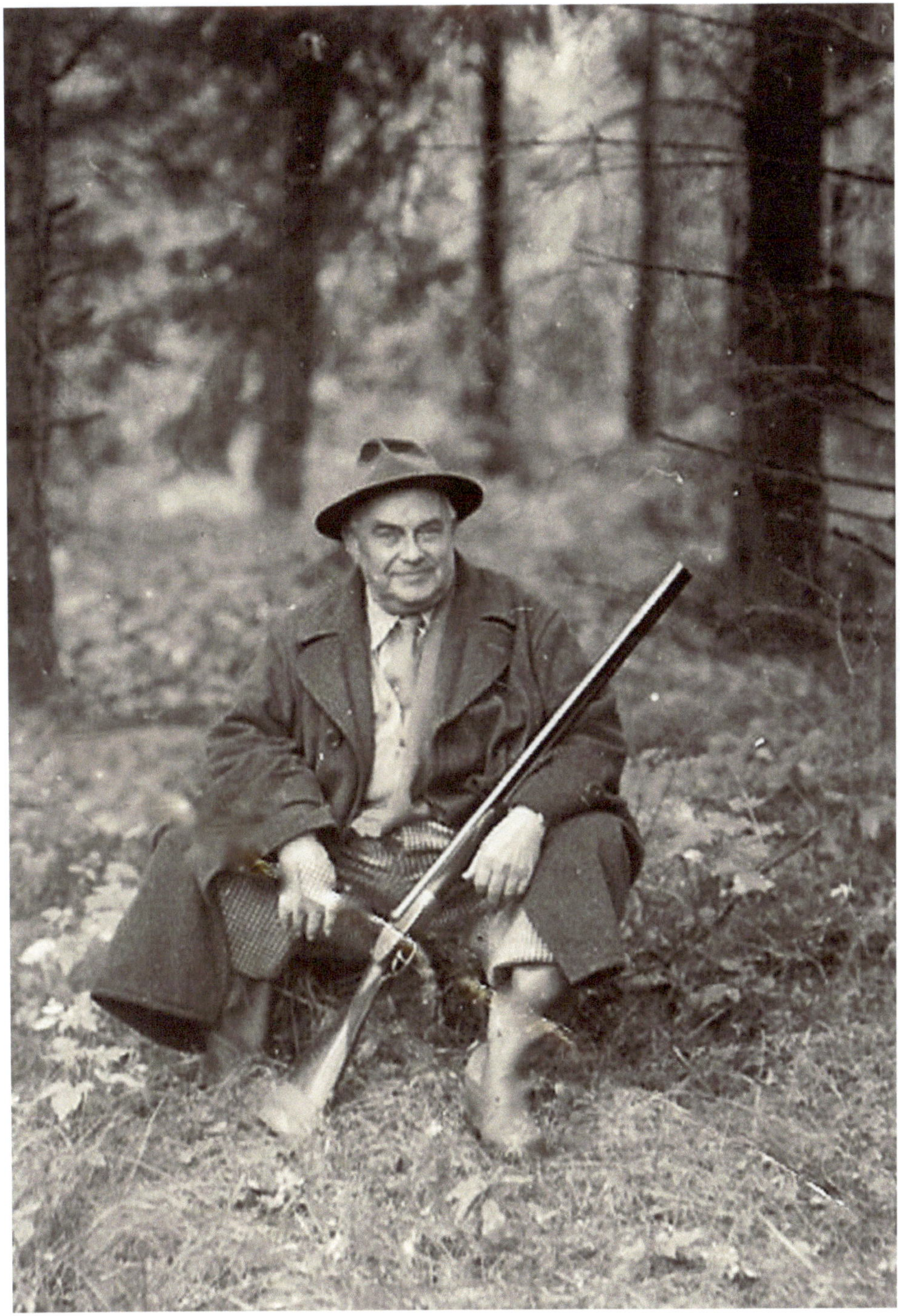

FOLKE HUNTING

Folke loved hunting.

He was an excellent shot and could fire his double barrel shotgun and fire another salvo in the same time as others would fire only once.

He belonged to a prominent hunting association in Gothenburg and often hosted their dinners at his hunting lodge Mååtorp in Fjärås Sweden. Folke and his nephew Sven Hansson kept six hunting dogs at Mååtorp.

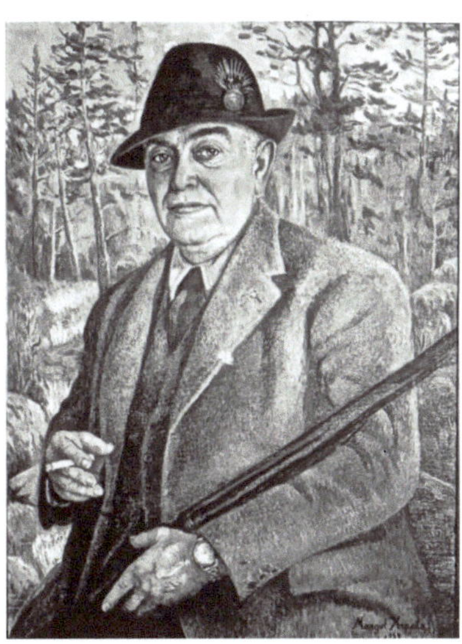

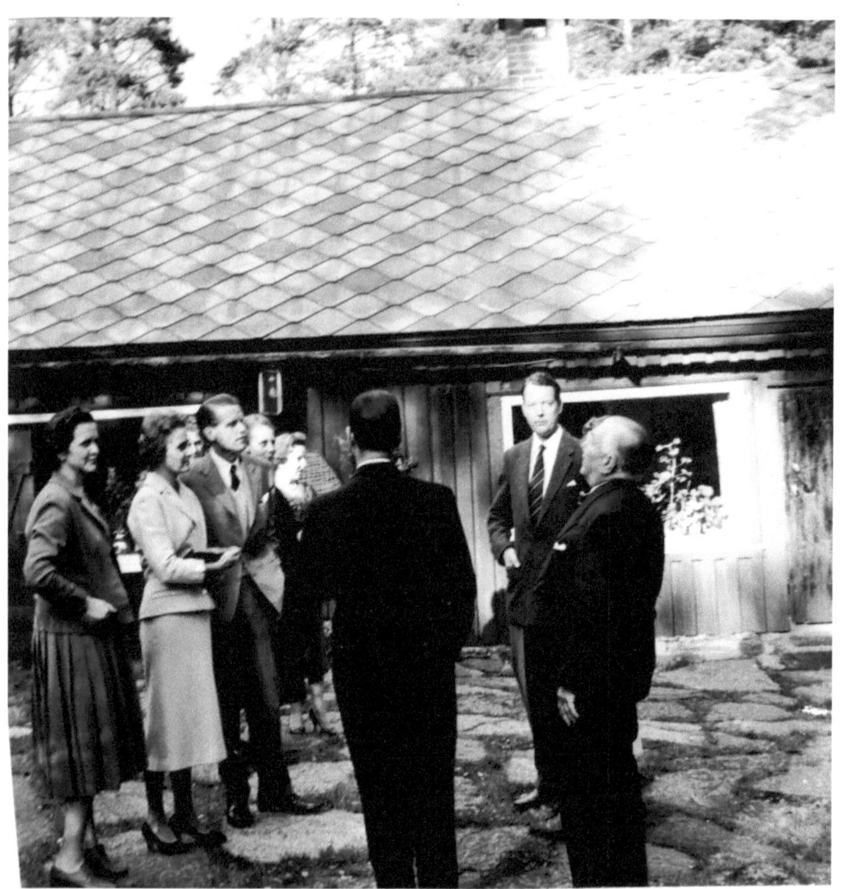

Folke bought a small cottage farm in 1946, deep in the forest near his hunting grounds in Fjärås, about an hour's drive from their house at Särö. By adding on and rebuilding the original cottage, he transformed it (taking a very active part in it himself) into a hunting lodge paradise. The surrounding garden and forest were turned into a wild park.

There were 6 hunting dogs, ducks, geese chickens and a large vegetable garden. In spring, the entire garden and the well kept forest exploded into colourful bulbs and coloured azalea and rhododendron bushes.

Folke was happy to have the marvelous Linnea (below). Cook, cleaner, seamtress, forest and general wonderworker, she could do nearly everything. With her, Folke could entertain very generously. It was a wonderful place to visit.

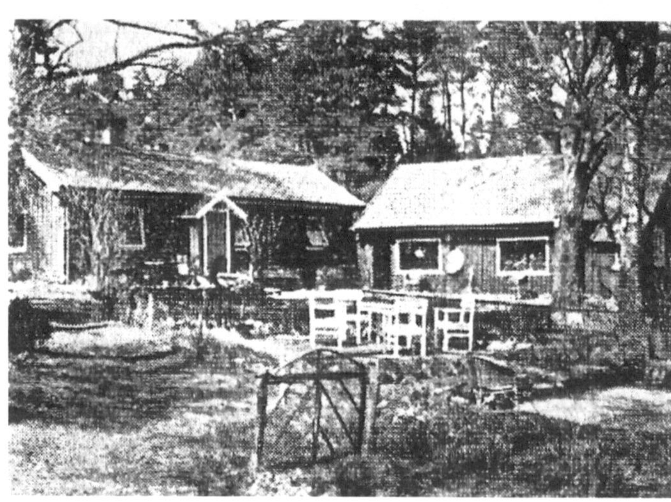

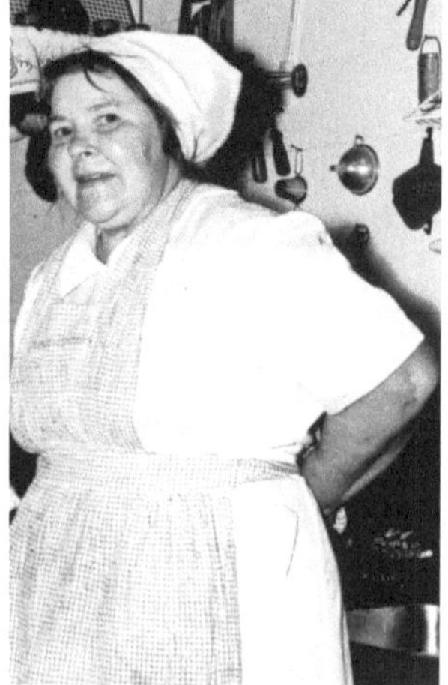

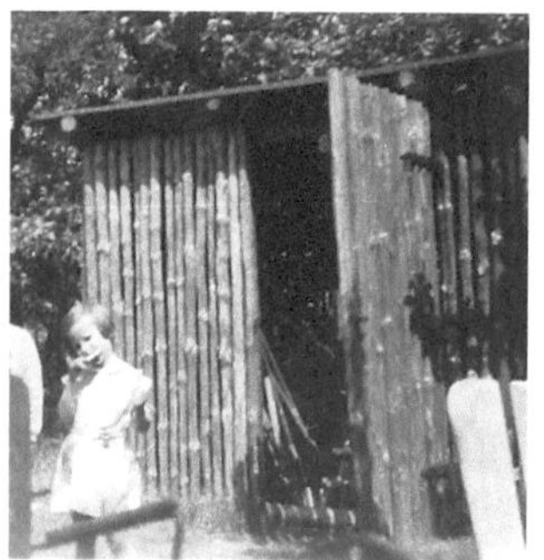

FOLKE'S MÅÅTORP

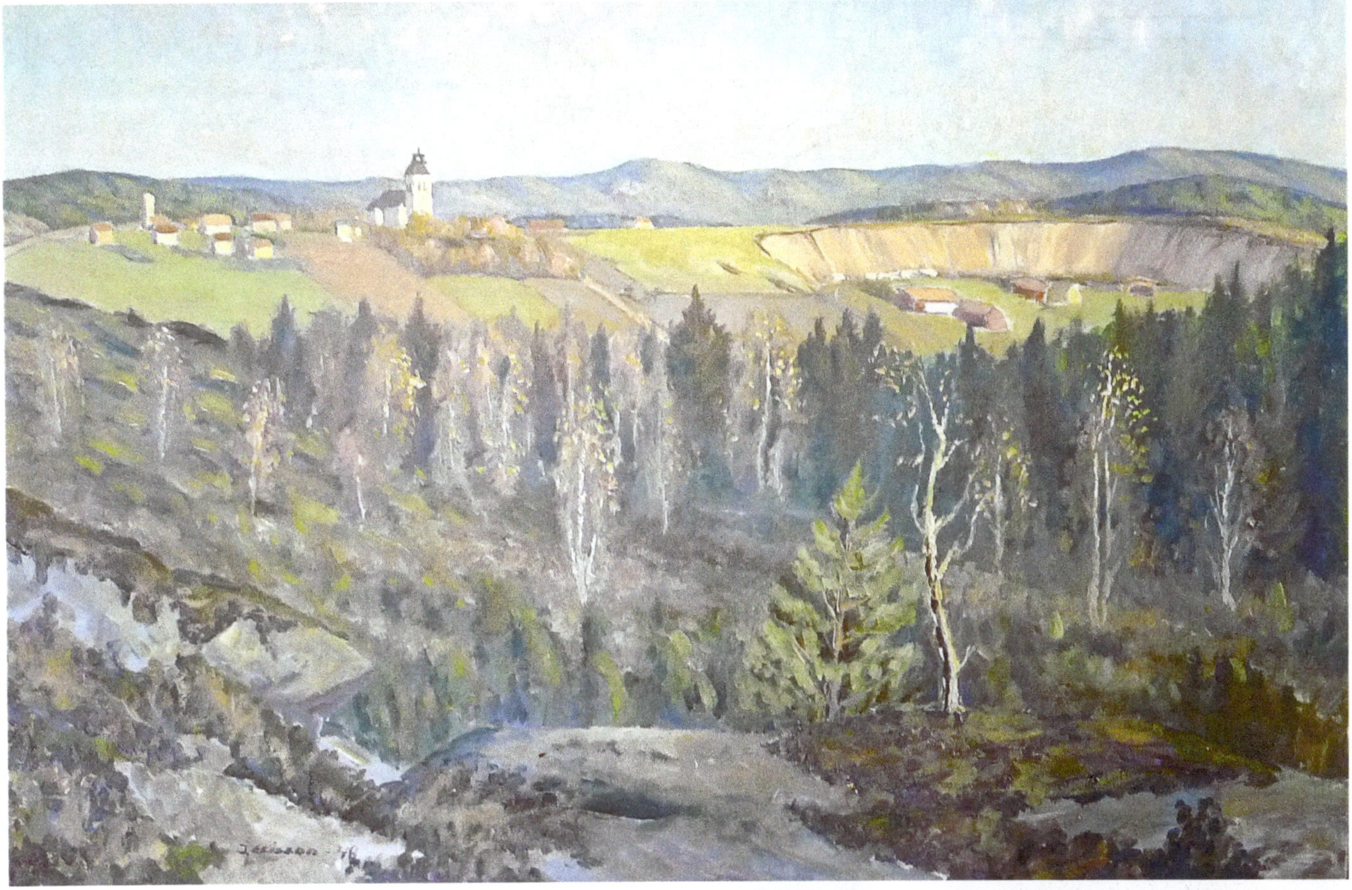

Above: This oil painting of "Fjärås Bräcka" by J. Ellison 1946, was in the living room at Måatorp.

Top left: Folke entertaining friends and relatives.

Bottom left: There were woodsheds and outbuildings built of slender tree trunks from the forest. Linnea, the cook helped to debark them with a double-handled tool made specially for her.

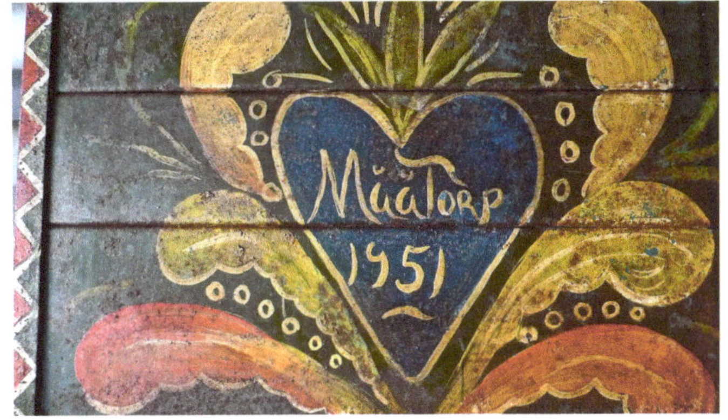

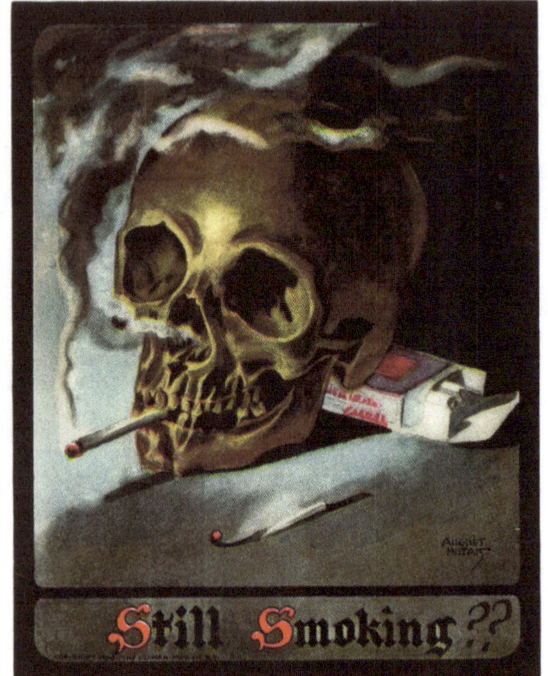

Friends and relatives remember Folke as a very happy man, fond of food, drink and smoking.

But in 1909 when Folke was only 23 years old and engaged to be married to his American Olga, she was determined he should not to smoke. She thought that by committing him to smoking only three cigarettes a day, this would eventually lead to him to stop altogether.

She kept after Folke as you can see from this humorous postcard (left). But this was no joke, Olga was dead serious in her anti-smoking effort. Folke wanting to please his young bride, did his best to keep to three cigarettes a day, and occasionally chose a pipe instead.

Almost every letter has some reference to this subject. But we know who won this fight...

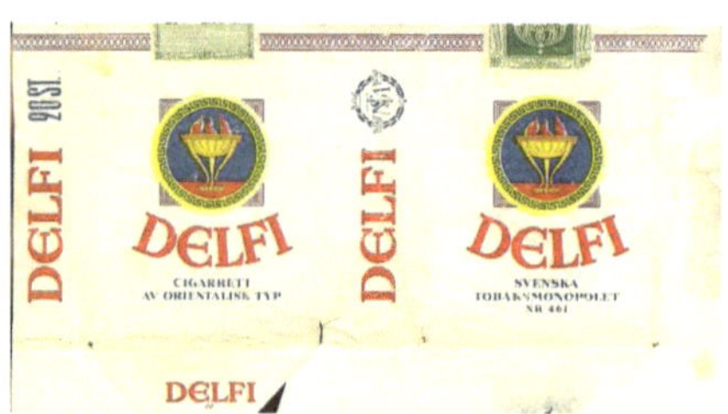

Folke's favourite cigarettes

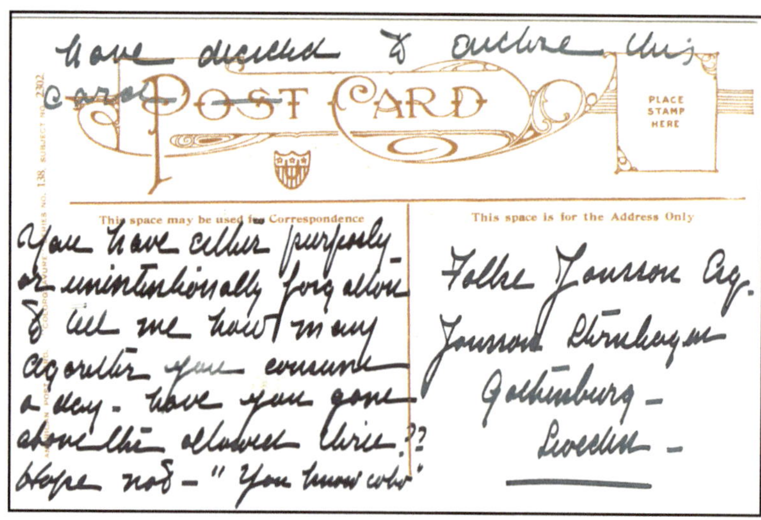
Have decided to answer this card

POST CARD

PLACE STAMP HERE

This space may be used for Correspondence

You have either purposely or unintentionally forgotten to tell me how many cigarettes you consume a day. Have you gone above the allowed three?? Hope not - "You know who"

This space is for the Address Only

Folke Jonsson Esq.

Gothenburg -

Sweden -

PLEASE, FOLKE, DON'T SMOKE...

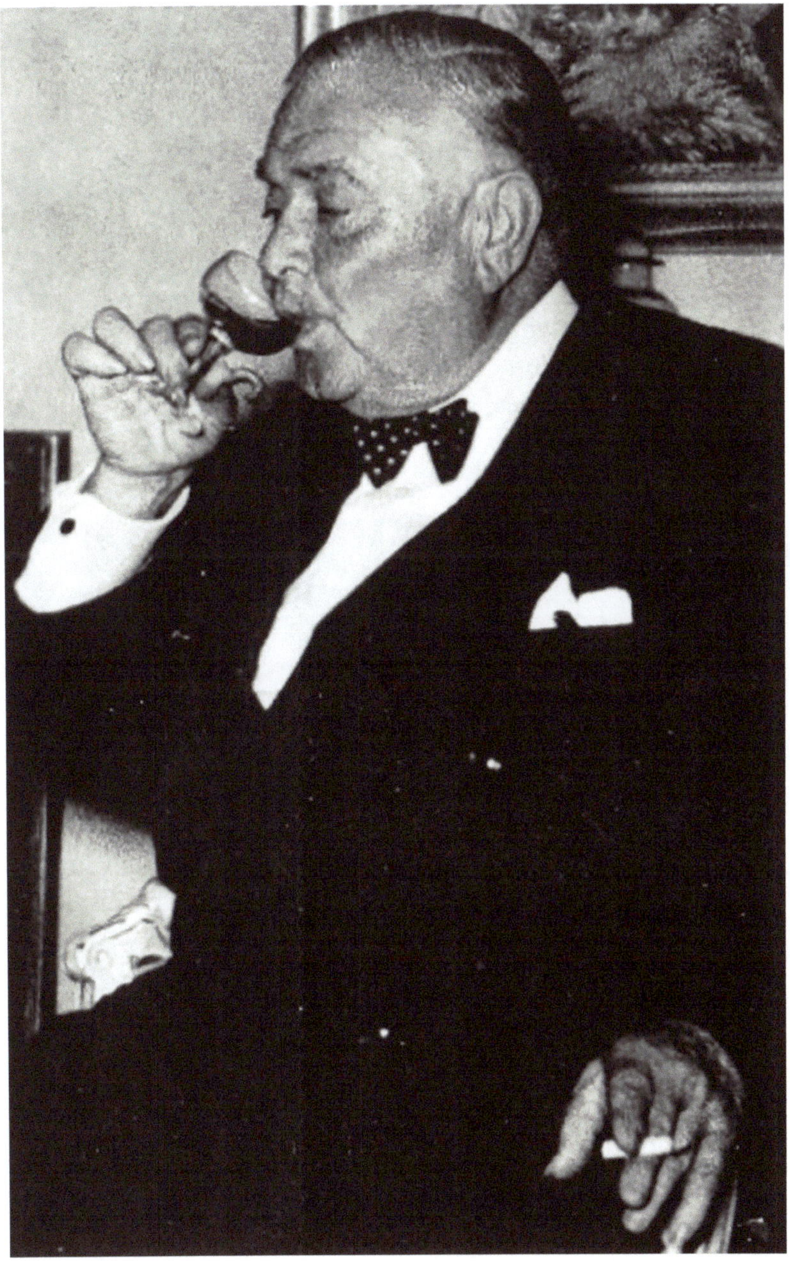

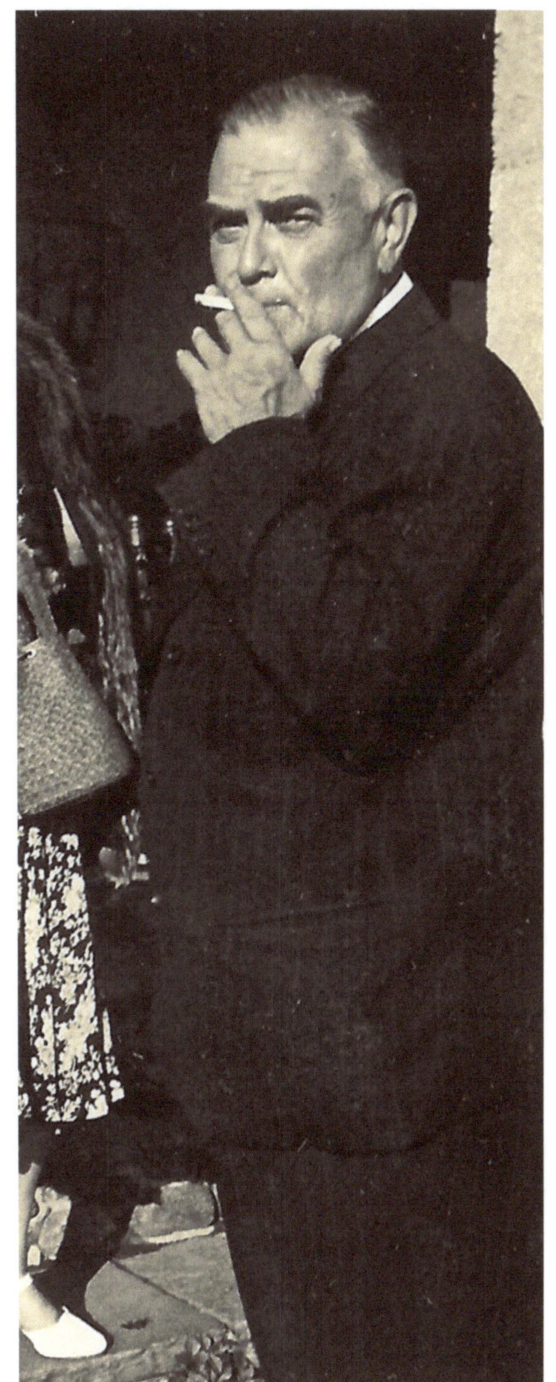

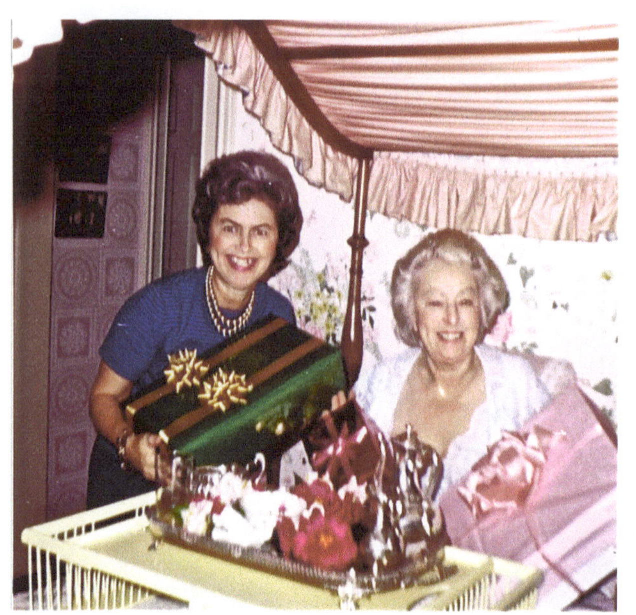

OLGA PAMPERED IN JACKSONVILLE

When Olga visited Florida, she stayed with her sister Una, or with her four children who were all living there. Here daughter Sigrid gives Olga breakfast in bed on her birthday (left).

Below:
1946 and WW2 is over. Olga can visit Florida for the first time since 1939. She has brought her daughter Mary with her and they are met in New York. (From left) Daughter Mary, Olga, daughter Sigrid with son Charles Jr. and husband Charles (who had come from Jacksonville to meet Olga and Mary in New York)

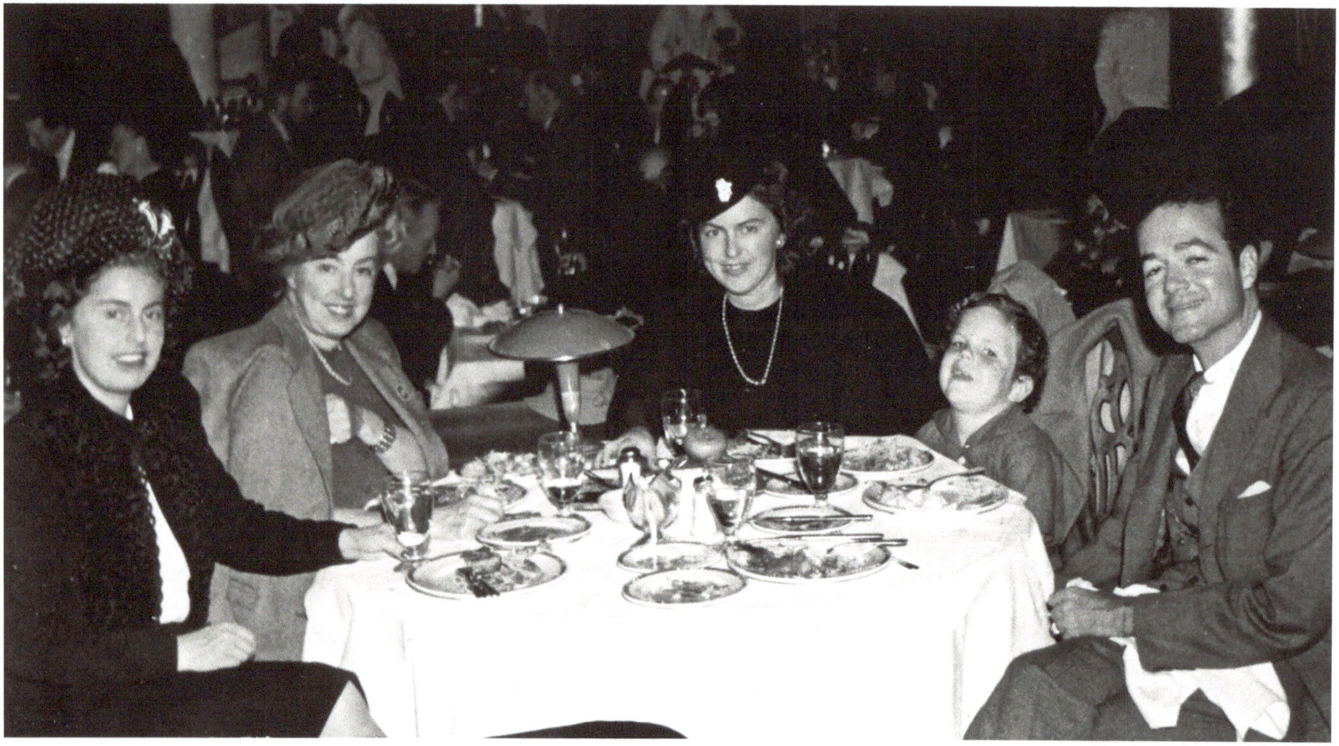

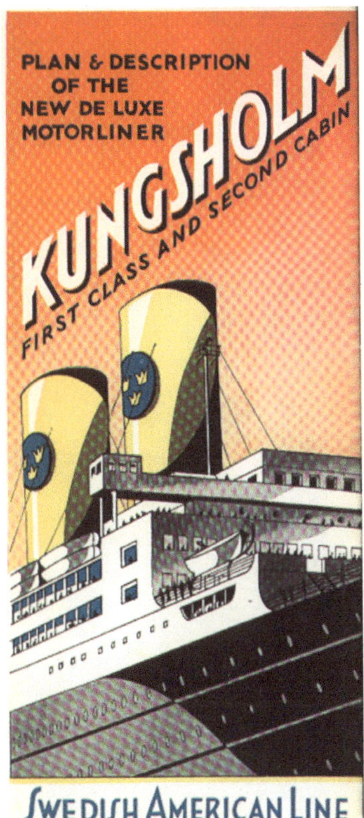

Olga and her family preferred The Swedish American Line. Fortunately, Folke's brother, Axel Jonsson, was the CEO there and could provide excellent help. The large cruise ships always left from Gothenburg. Olga then took a train from New York to Florida.

Travels to Florida

Olga, being American, had her family in Florida and Folke soon came to realize that if you marry a woman from another continent, and this woman is charmingly independent, innovative and brave, and has her own means to boot, she is bound to visit her native country some time -- or several times -- or more than several times.

Olga most often travelled on one of the large passenger ships, but there were alternatives. Here she is in 1963, on a freighter with daughter Gunilla. This small freighter took a few passengers only, and went from Gothenburg to Jacksonville stopping in many ports on the way. This was convenient for Olga who shopped at each port -- her cabin was often stuffed full with gifts. Remember, dear reader, Olga and Folke had four children living in America and five children in Sweden. All had growing families, and, happily, Olga was the loving mother and grandmother of them all!

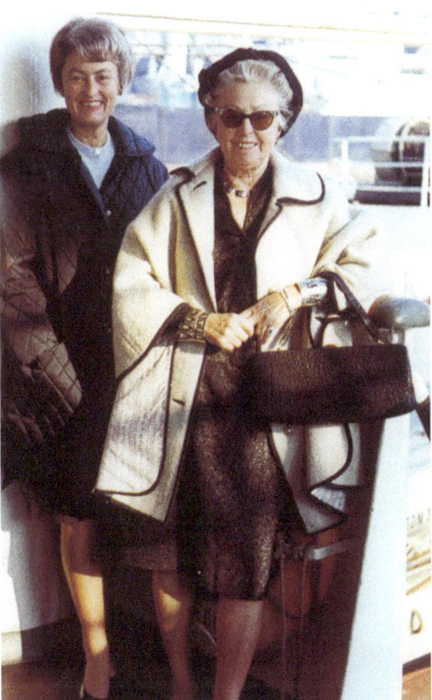

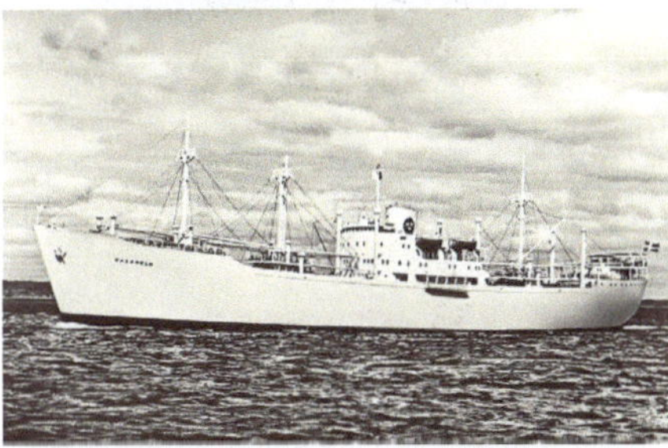

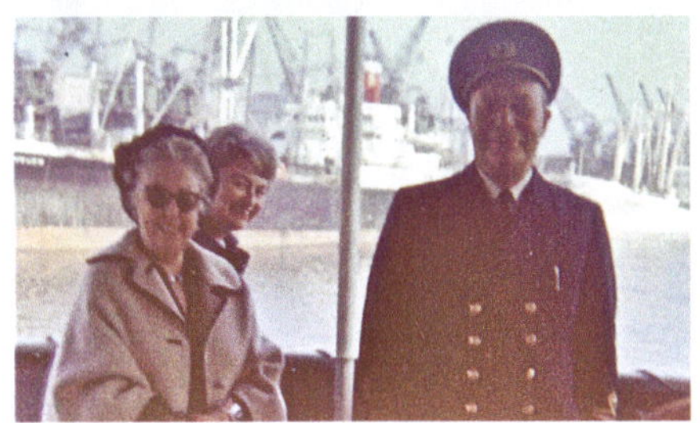

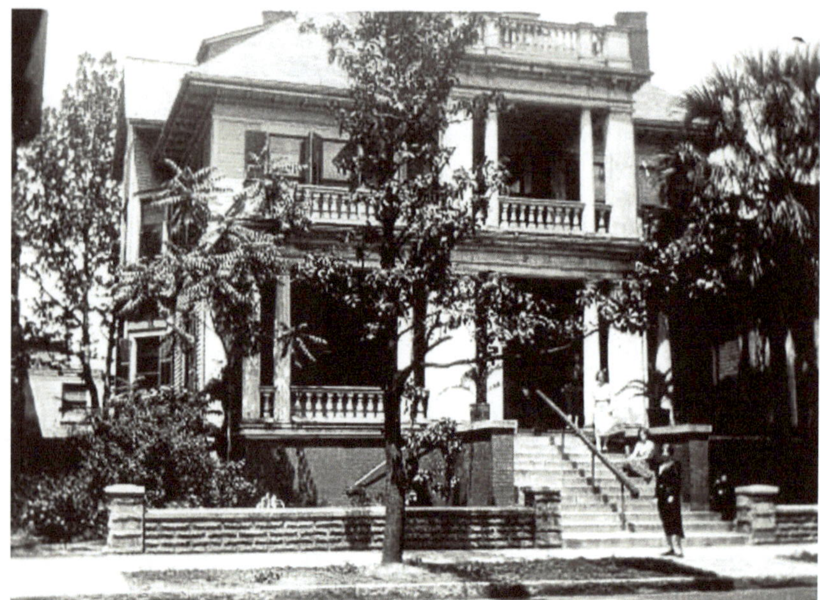

Olga's parents' home on 115 East Adams Street in Jacksonville, Florida. This is where Folke's letters arrived in 1913, when he wrote for many months, hoping Olga would come home for Christmas.

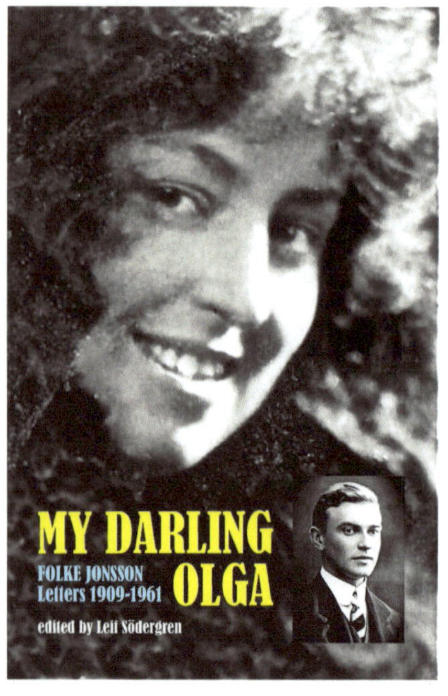

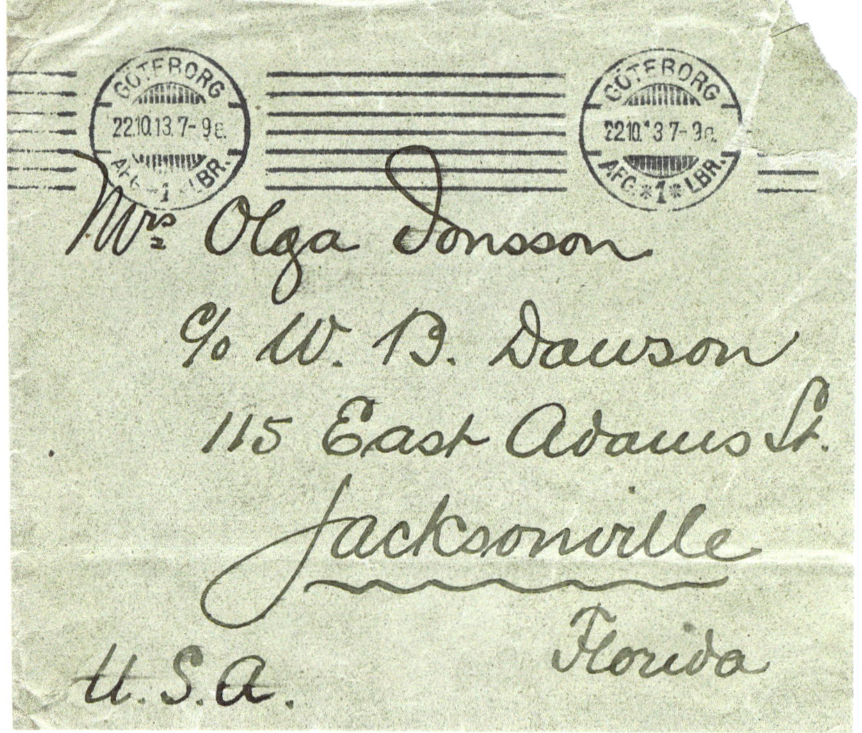

FOLKE'S LETTERS

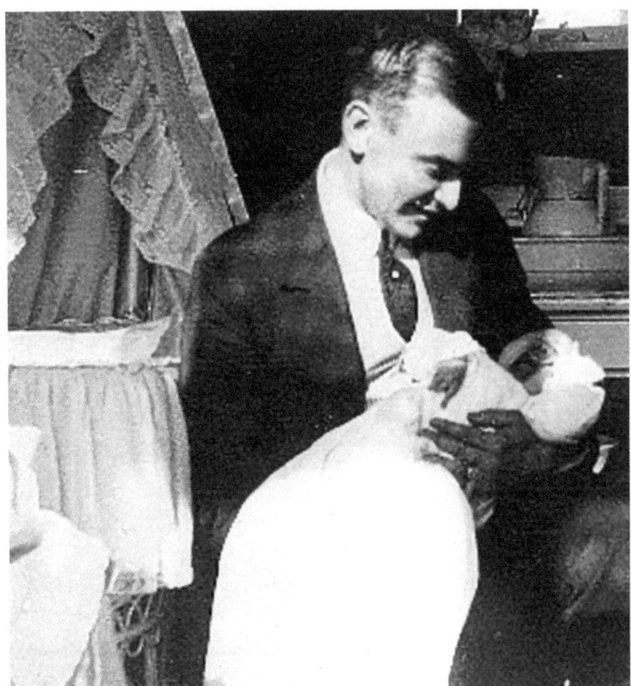

Folke alone at home in Gothenburg, Sweden with baby Mary Carita in 1913.

Olga was usually gone for several months during each visit to Florida. It is said that absence makes the heart grow fonder, but to Folke, a sensitive soul, the long separations were quite painful. He was miserable till his darling Olga returned.

He "talked" to her in his frequent letters when she was absent. The letters were always dated, the pages perfectly numbered and in the finest handwriting -- a joy to read. He never intended the letters to be shown to others, but more than one hundred years have passed since Folke wrote them.

Had my grandfather Folke married a Swedish woman who had stayed at home, we would not have this valuble intimate history today.

FOOD FIT FOR A KING

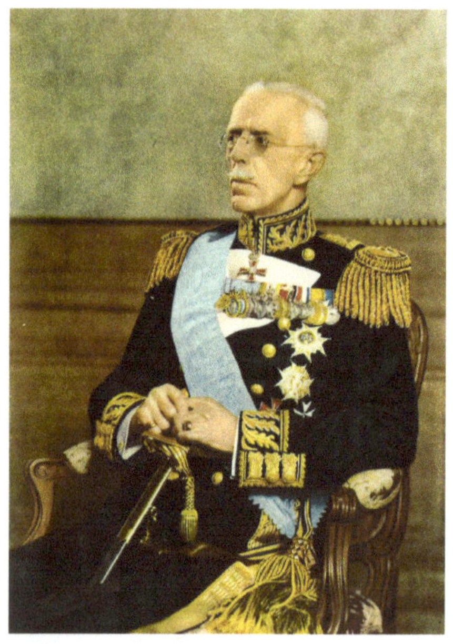

The Swedish King Gustav V, a regular visitor every summer, loved Linnea's food. She was the best cook ever, he thought, and said he couldn't get any better food in his own palace in Stockholm. He always kept a fresh supply of her sweet crisp rolls (socker-skorpor).

The King's signature is engraved in granite at Lysholmen (lower left)

Linnea loved to work outdoors too, as well as all the cooking, cleaning and washing. She also did not shy away from mowing the lawn, raking or helping Folke debark trees in the forest. She was quite unusual, a happy phenomenon. She would bathe Olga, in Olga's old age, with the most tender care. When Linnea was in her late 60s, she grew tomatoes in the Lysholmen greenhouse. She had a local farmer deliver horse manure every spring and she moved it into the greenhouse with a wheel barrow. She was proud of her large crop of tomatoes every year as well as all the lettuce and peaches.

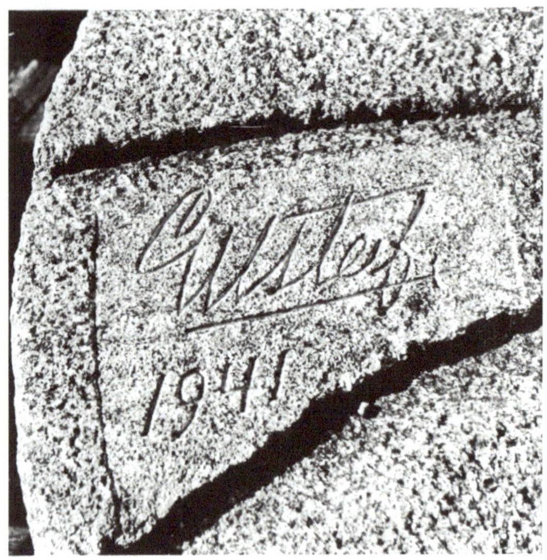

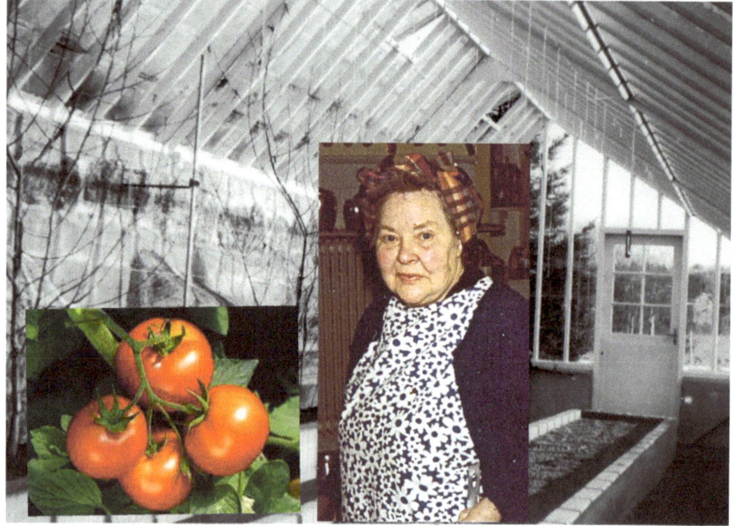

AND LAST, BUT NOT LEAST : **AMAZING LINNEA !**

Linnea could always whip up a fine dinner when surprise visitors were invited, a common occurrence. She was a master, but the kitchen was her domain and she would tolerate no interference. She did not use a washing machine or a dishwasher and always had the copper and silver shining to perfection.

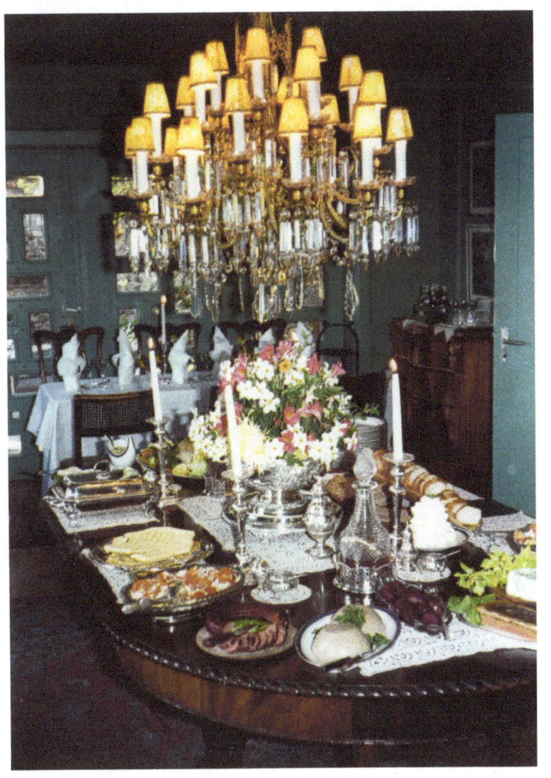

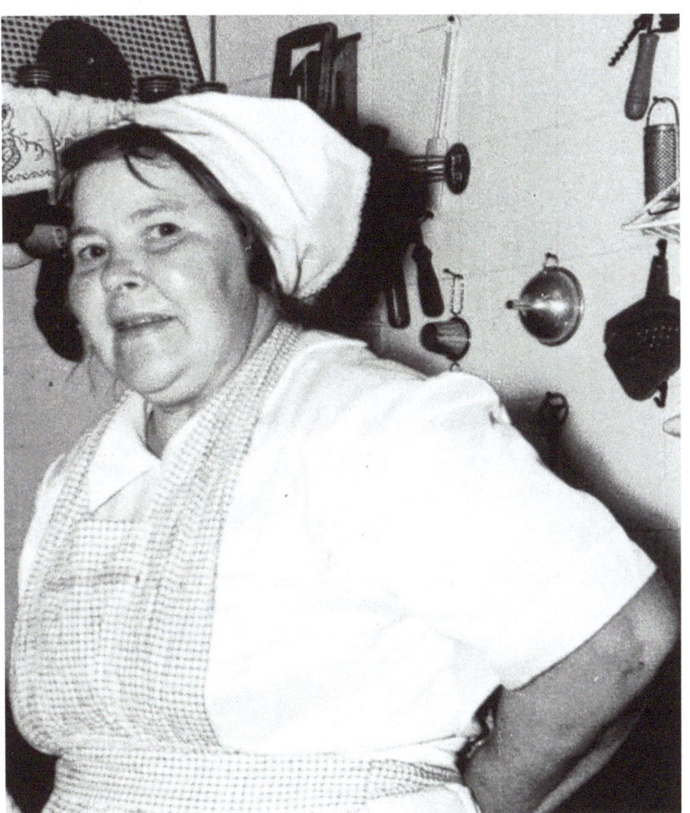

The nearly super-human "Linnea", was enormously loyal and devoted to my grandparents. She stayed with them as long as they both lived, and guaranteed in their later days, that Folke and Olga could live a life that very few enjoyed. Linnea would never have stayed with them for almost 40 years had she not felt happy and at home. She was deeply valued by both Olga and Folke as well as the entire family.

FAMILY FACTS

OLGA MIMS (DAWSON) JONSSON 1890 - 1978

FOLKE JONSSON 1886 - 1961

THEIR CHILDREN:
Anita 1910
Billy 1911
Mary 1913
Sonja 1915
Sigrid 1917
Bo-Erling 1918
Gunilla 1921
Ponkis (Folke) 1922
Claes-Herbert 1930

OLGA'S PARENTS:
Anita (Ball) Dawson 1858 - 1931
William Dawson 1856 - 1916

FOLKE'S PARENTS:
Ragnhild (Lundgren) Jonsson 1864 - 1903
Axel Jonsson 1844-1931

THE AUTHOR

Leif Södergren is the grandson of Folke and Olga Jonsson. He grew up in and now lives in Gothenburg, Sweden.

He has a B.A. and Master of Arts Degree in American Studies at California State University, San Diego.

He has worked with International Marine Insurance for many years.

He now works with publishing, writing, and has had one Swedish and one English blog since 2009.

Like his grandmother Olga, he also paints Swedish Folk Art.

www.ingramcontent.com/pod-product-compliance
Lightning Source LLC
LaVergne TN
LVHW070144110826
845147LV00002B/326